The Laird's Kitchen

David Allan, 'While Peggy laces up her bosom fair', in Allan Ramsay, The Gentle Shepherd
(Edinburgh, 1788).
National Library of Scotland.

The Laird's Kitchen

Three Hundred Years of Food in Scotland

Olive M. Geddes

EDINBURGH: HMSO

THE NATIONAL LIBRARY OF SCOTLAND

First published 1994

Designed by Derek Munn, HMSO Scotland Graphic Design
Principal photography by Sam Sloan
Additional Photography by HMSO Scotland and Steve McAvoy of the National Library of Scotland
Food styling and propping by Wendy Barrie

British Library Cataloguing in Publication Data

A catalogue record for this book is available from the British Library

ACKNOWLEDGEMENTS

In preparing this book, I have been greatly helped by a number of colleagues and authorities. In particular, I would like to thank Annette Hope, who gave generously of her wealth of knowledge on Scottish food history. Thanks are also due for her detailed commentary on the entire manuscript. Her criticisms and suggestions improved the text immeasurably. The National Trust for Scotland was most helpful and co-operative. Rosalind K. Marshall of the Scottish National Portrait Gallery provided many helpful suggestions for illustrations. I would also like to thank my mother, Margaret Riding, who tested many of the recipes. My colleagues in the National Library of Scotland, particularly Kenneth Gibson and Jacqueline Cromarty of the Publications Division, also Margaret Wilkes, Iain Brown, Louise Yeoman and Jess Blower, have been supportive throughout.
I would also like to thank the many private individuals and institutions who have allowed me to reproduce photographs of their documents, paintings and culinary equipment: their names are to be found in the captions.

Lady Grisell Baillie's coffee pot and jug on page 38, the tea cup and saucer on page 39, the skillet on page 45, the soup plate on page 62, the claret jug on page 87, the fish slice on page 94, and the sugar nips on page 96, appear courtesy of the National Museums of Scotland; the cutlery box on page 89, and the glassware on page 90, are reproduced courtesy of the National Trust for Scotland; the Scottish standards on page ix, the silver teapot and sugar bowl on page 38, and the silver gilt dessert baskets on page 100, appear courtesy of Huntly House Museum, Edinburgh.
The untitled illustrations on pages 6, 7, 8, 17 and 48 are from Blaeu's *Atlas* (Amsterdam, 1653); those on page 102 are from Isabella Beeton, *The Book of Household Management* (London, 1869); and the cattle and sheep on pages 21 and 47 are from William Daniell, *A Voyage Round Great Britain* (London, 1814).

ISBN 0 11 495230 2

CONTENTS

Acknowledgements · iv

Introduction · vii

Scots Weights and Measures · ix

1 · Menschotts and Wine: Glasgow, 1608 · 1

2 · Marmalade, Haggis and Potatoes: Sutherland, 1683-1712 · 15

3 · Sausages, Tea and Barley: Saltoun, 1688-1716 · 31

4 · Sheep's Head Broth and Oysters: Ochtertyre, 1737-1739 · 43

5 · Cookery Schools and Cheesecakes: Edinburgh, 1752-1758 · 57

6 · Trifle, Curry and Rhubarb: Burnfoot, 1782-1813 · 71

7 · Turkey Figs, American Apples and Dutch Cheese: Bowland, 1836-1860 · 85

8 · Chocolate, Tomatoes and Crappit Heids: 1847-1910 · 99

Selected Further Reading · 108

Index · 109

Katharine Jane Ellice, 'Etta Making His Toast', 1854.
National Library of Scotland, MS.15172, no.6.

INTRODUCTION

Some live to eat, others eat to live. Food is essential to life for us all, but that does not mean we all eat the same things prepared in the same way and at the same times. This is as true today as it ever was. When the Minister of Rousay and Egilsay in Orkney reported in his return for *The Statistical Account of Scotland* of the 1790s that 'There is no difference in the manners and habits between the cottager and the master . . . They all take social snuff together', his surprised tone suggests that this was highly unusual.[1]

In Scotland, as elsewhere, in times of prosperity, those who owned land could afford to eat better, both in terms of quality and quantity, than those who did not. In times of harvest failure, rich and poor alike suffered. The rich were generally better educated, had a repertoire of dishes to choose from, and employed servants to run their households. They were, therefore, in a position to compile recipe books, and were motivated to keep accounts of household expenditure. The poor in their hovels left no such record of their lives: we may open the doors of the kitchens and dining rooms of the wealthy, but those of the poor remain closed.

The archives of many important families include details of their eating habits, providing a remarkable insight into both their private and public lives. Inevitably, these are fragmentary. Some families kept detailed records, others took a more haphazard approach, and of course many documents have been lost over the years. Consequently, such records alone are not reliable sources for food history, and must be supplemented by a study of the period from diaries, letters and papers describing actual cooking and eating habits. Recipe books, in particular, have their limitations as sources.[2]

Manuscript recipe books are personal documents. Written mostly by aristocratic and later middle-class women, these are memory aids in which new culinary experiences were noted. Few housewives took the trouble to write down recipes for dishes in everyday use: such knowledge would be transmitted orally. Moreover, at many times and in many households it was not considered seemly for a gently-born woman to concern herself with the daily toil of food provision beyond the supervision of her servants. Those recipes worthy of her note might be for preserves (gathering and preserving produce from the garden and orchard were generally thought fitting tasks for ladies), delicacies for special occasions, and novelties. Often, recipe books have more than one author, being passed from mother to daughter and one generation to another.

Printed recipe books are compiled for different reasons. Unless they are intentionally specialised, they cover the entire range of dishes served in a wealthy household. The authors are usually experienced cooks, both male and female, seeking to pass on their knowledge to others and to generate income. While manu-

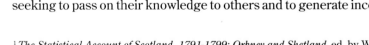

---

[1] *The Statistical Account of Scotland, 1791-1799: Orkney and Shetland*, ed. by W. P. L. Thomson and J. J. Graham (1978), XIX, p. 199.

[2] Edith Horandner, 'The Recipe Book as a Cultural and Socio-Historical Document', in *Food in Perspective,* ed. by Alexander Fenton and Trefor M. Owen (Edinburgh, 1981), pp. 119-44.

script recipe books tend to reflect current trends, printed recipe books are often outdated by the time of publication.

Recipe books rarely give the source of foodstuffs: whether home-grown on the estate, in the kitchen garden or orchard; bought in from a wandering tradesman, merchant or shop; or, until the early nineteenth century, acquired as rent from tenants. This deficiency may be remedied by household account books and vouchers recording incoming and sometimes outgoing supplies.

Further invaluable information can be gleaned from diet books, detailing dishes served at specific meals in particular households, and bills of fare, recording actual or ideal meals. However, these records, too, have their limitations: quantities are rarely stated, and they usually omit to note how many people are being catered for. Leaving aside these limitations, they are important source materials. Unfortunately, diet books and bills of fare are all too rare, making comparison between contemporary households difficult if not impossible.

Scotland has not been as fortunate as her European neighbours in the compilation and survival of records relating to food history. Indeed, little at all exists before the late sixteenth century. However, a number of sources from the family archives of Scotland's lairds survive among the manuscripts in the National Library of Scotland. Using these materials, and bearing in mind the reservations noted above, it is possible to build up a picture of the diet and eating habits of the wealthier members of Scottish society over a period of some three hundred years.

Scots Weights and Measures

Sets of standards for weights and measures were first introduced in Scotland in 1457 in Edinburgh, Perth and Aberdeen. In 1503, Edinburgh was recognised as the centre for standards, and in 1618 James VI made a determined effort to establish a single standard for the entire country. In spite of his attempts, local standards persisted in many areas. Officially, Scottish standards for weights and measures were abolished with the Act of Union of 1707. However, uniformity still proved difficult to achieve, with the old systems often operating alongside Imperial measures well into the nineteenth century: in some rural areas they were still in occasional use in the early years of the twentieth century.

The lack of a nationally accepted set of standards means that it is often difficult to establish which standards were in use in a particular location at a given time. It is also often difficult to ascertain whether stated measures are Scots or Imperial. Similarly, many household accounts use pounds Scots (one Scots shilling was worth roughly one penny sterling) while others use pounds sterling. In many cases it is difficult to tell which is which.

The following equivalents must be taken as a rough guide only.

Scots	Imperial	Metric
Liquid capacity		
gallon	3 gallons	13.638 litres
pint	3 pints	1.696 litres
chopin	2 pints	0.848 litres
mutchkin	3/4 pint	0.212 litres
Dry capacity		
forpet or lippie	0.499 gallons	2.268 litres
peck	1.996 gallons	9.072 litres
weight		
drop	1.093 drams	1.921 grammes
ounce	1 ounce 1.5 drams	31 grammes
lib	1 pound 1 ounce 8 drams	496 grammes

1 MENSCHOTTS AND WINE

GLASGOW, 1608

ON TUESDAY, 19 JULY 1608, JOHN ROSS'S LODGING HOUSE IN GLASGOW HAD A DISTINGUISHED clientele, as among his lodgers were William Douglas, Earl of Angus, his Countess, Elizabeth, their family and servants. That day the household dined alone, consuming no less than three beef 'staiks' (steaks), five veal steaks, eight mutton steaks, six chickens, and two 'powts' (pullets), as well as forty menschotts (small loaves or rolls of the finest wheaten flour, otherwise known as manchet), twenty-one loaves of oat bread, three pints of French wine, and the same of ale.[1] Considered a threat to the stability of the nation because of his religious beliefs, the Earl had been ordered to remain in Glasgow. By mid-July 1608 he had been in residence for over five weeks.

Daily accounts of the Earl's household expenditure, largely but not entirely on foodstuffs, have survived for the five months between 11 June and 19 November 1608, for all save the final month of which the Earl and his family were in Glasgow. Noting daily purchases of supplies for the kitchen and the buttery, the quantities of foodstuffs issued, amounts remaining in store, and the total daily expenditure on provisions, the accounts represent an apparently complete record of one aristocratic household's expenditure on food.

William Douglas, 10th Earl of Angus, was born in about 1554.[2] As a young man, he studied at St Andrews University, and in 1575 entered the service of the Regent Morton. In 1577, he attended the court of King Henry III of France to complete his education. Although in the mid-sixteenth century the Italians led the way in culinary expertise and innovation, the cuisine of the French court was nevertheless far more sophisticated than anything William Douglas would have experienced in Scotland, and must have made an impression on him.

Whatever the effect of the cuisine, while in France Douglas was converted to Roman Catholicism. Returning to Scotland in 1580, the Earl's new-found religious beliefs alienated not only his father, but also the Privy Council of Scotland, to such an extent that he was ordered to leave the country. This he failed to do on the grounds that he was unable to find a ship. In 1591, the Earl was ordered to Stirling Castle. However, on the death of his father in the summer of that year, he successfully petitioned to be allowed to live in Edinburgh.

Notwithstanding the considerable restrictions imposed on him over the years, Douglas held high office, being appointed King's Lieutenant and Justice-General north of the Tay in 1592. Later, he became Lieutenant for the entire Scottish Borders. Nevertheless, the persecution for his beliefs continued. Alleged involve-

Coat of Arms of the Earls of Angus from the Seton Armorial, 1591. National Library of Scotland, Acc.9309. By permission of Sir Francis Ogilvy.

[1] National Library of Scotland, MS.2200, ff.1-58. See Alexander O. Curle, 'The Kitchen and Buttery Accounts of the Earl of Angus's Household, in Glasgow and the Canongate . . . 1608', *Proceedings of the Society of Antiquaries of Scotland*, 42 (1908), 191-207.

[2] For a detailed discussion of the life of William, 10th Earl of Angus, see Sir William Fraser, *The Douglas Book*, 4 vols (Edinburgh, 1885).

ment in the Popish Plot known as the 'Spanish Blanks' led to imprisonment in Edinburgh Castle from which, with the assistance of his Countess, Elizabeth Oliphant, he escaped to the north of Scotland. Once there, Douglas and the other Roman Catholic Earls, Atholl and Huntly, openly defied the King. In spite of his later reconciliation with the King and the Kirk, Douglas continued in his beliefs, with the result that his persecution was renewed, and in 1608 the Kirk insisted he go into ward once again – this time in Glasgow.

In the early 1600s, Glasgow was growing rapidly in both size and status. In 1556, the tax assessments of the Convention of the Royal Burghs of Scotland, the most reliable indicators of the relative prosperity of Scottish towns, had listed Glasgow as eleventh behind Ayr. In little over a century, her expansion was such that she was second only to Edinburgh in the amount of tax paid by her citizens.[3]

Detail from Timothy Pont's map of Glasgow and Lanarkshire, 1596. In the Middle Ages, Glasgow was one of the smaller of the Scottish trading burghs. When the Earl of Angus was in residence in 1608, it was growing rapidly in both size and status. *National Library of Scotland, Pont.34.*

Favourably situated on the Clyde estuary in the centre of Scotland, Glasgow was at the crossroads of several major arteries, her prosperity already firmly based on commerce. In 1578, Bishop Lesley wrote, 'Surely Glasgow is the maist renowned market in all the west, honourable and celebrate . . . it sends to the Easte cuntreyes [eastern Scotland] vere fatt kye [cows], herring, lykwyse and salmonte [salmon], oxenhydes, wole [wool] and skinis, butter lykwyse that nane bettir and chiese [cheese]'.[4] Glasgow was also the centre for the despatch of corn westwards to Argyll and the Highlands and Islands. Wine and ale were sent to 'the outermost Isles of Ireland'. The city's international trade, notably exports of Scottish fish and imported French salt and wine, was still in its infancy.

In spite of Glasgow's prosperity and the intellectual stimulus of its university, Douglas found the city a particularly objectionable place in which to live. Even before his arrival he petitioned the King that he be allowed to stay on the east coast for the sake of his health. Glasgow, he wrote, 'was a place verie unmeit for me for sindrie respectis but speciallie for recouverie of my healthe'.[5] Douglas's plea went unanswered and the family duly moved west.

Saturday 11 June 1608, when the Earl of Angus's accounts proper begin, was the date of the family's move to John Ross's 'lugging' (lodging house). This was not their first home in Glasgow, as the accounts open with the payment of £39 to George Lyonn for 'thrie nights for chalmer mail, fyre, and candill'. So, for the rent money, the landlord supplied furnished rooms, heating and candles. His lodgers made their own arrangements for food and drink.

As is the case with many such records, the accounts do have their limitations. In particular, the numbers of both family and servants making up the Earl's household can only be guessed at. However, meal given to the dogs and chickens, and beef fed to the hawks suggest a large establishment, if in somewhat straitened circumstances. Marginal notes record the names of visitors and the hospitality accorded them, making it possible to distinguish between the everyday fare provided for the household and that for special occasions.

[3] T. Christopher Smout, 'The Development and Enterprise of Glasgow, 1556-1707', *Scottish Journal of Political Economy*, 7 (1960), 194-212.

[4] P. Hume Brown, *Scotland before 1700 from Contemporary Documents* (Edinburgh, 1893), pp. 120-1.

[5] Fraser, IV, p.192.

Household accounts of William, 10th Earl of Angus, 1608.
Daily accounts of food eaten by the Earl of Angus's household over five months in 1608 have survived.
National Library of Scotland, MS.2200, f.31.

Waidinesdey ye Last dey of august

Enterit of menschottis _____ *iiii*ˣˣ
Enterit of aitt bred _____ *iiii*ˣˣ
Enterit of aill & cost _ xvi qrts _____ *Restes xviiish*
Enterit of frensche wyne __ iii poynts ___ xxxiiish
Enterit of canerie wyne ane choipin ____ *viiish*

Spendit

In me[n]schottis ____ *Li* _____ *Restes iiixx xv*
In aitt bred _____ *xxx* _____ *Restes L*
In aill _____ *xvi gl [gallons]* _____ *Restes*
In wyne _____ *iii poynt* _____ *Restes*

Ketchein

Enterit & cost ane mowttoun bowik __ xxxvish ane half
half hunderᵗ hereng __ vish viiid Thre dosoun aiges __ xsh
vid beir and herbeis __ iiiish fower candill __ viiish
anepoynt wyneger __ viiish
ane leid of collis __ xsh

Su[mm]a viiilib iish iid

Since the family's ancestral home, Douglas Castle near Lanark, was several hours' ride on horseback away, most of the provisions for the household were bought in. Sources of bought goods are given only infrequently. When they do appear, the names are those of local merchants. Baxters (bakers) are named, as are the milk-wife, and the wine merchant. In some respects Glasgow merchants, as indeed the city generally, must have failed to live up to the Earl's standards, as the accounts show family and servants on business in Edinburgh returning with supplies of bread. The implication is that they had been primed to visit specific merchants and tradesmen there.

Some of the meat eaten by the family came on the hoof from Douglas Castle. Other supplies sent from Douglas were chickens, geese, cheese, and butter. These foodstuffs could all be obtained in Glasgow and there is no doubt that the family could well afford to buy them. However, as the Earl was head of the house of Douglas, these provisions were his by right. They may well have been sent to him in 'exile' as a means of demonstrating his continuing dominance of the family. Given the distance from Glasgow, they could not have been sent as an economy measure. Other items, such as pairs of rabbits, from the Douglas stronghold of Tantallon Castle in East Lothian, were brought as gifts by grateful visitors.

Usually, the exiled family received donations of meat, poultry and game, but from time to time they dispensed surplus food to others. Most frequently this happened when bread was brought back from Edinburgh. Once, the Countess gave away eleven score bread rolls on a single day. When ten 'cheip [sheep] of my Lord's awin' arrived from Douglas, four of the animals were slaughtered the next day. Presumably, they were either eaten fresh or preserved for future consumption. Another four were despatched to Tantallon. No explanation is given for this, but as the family was living in temporary lodgings, perhaps they were simply unable to deal with such a large quantity of meat.

The accounts show a diet heavily dominated by flesh, and in particular by beef. In the Middle Ages, animal-derived foodstuffs had been important in the diet of the majority of Scots, common people and laird alike. Although the evidence is scanty, the Scots diet then consisted of largely of meat, cheese, butter, and milk. By the early seventeenth century, a noticeable change had taken place.[6] While the lairds continued to eat meat, the poor now had a grain-based diet. Eating copious amounts of flesh had become an indicator of wealth and status.

Usually bought by the side or the leg, the amount of beef served to the Earl of Angus was recorded by the number of steaks. One leg of beef could yield as many as sixteen steaks. The accounts of items taken from the larder show that beef and veal were served almost daily. Mutton and lamb, too, came by the carcase or side. Poultry, in the form of chickens or capons, was purchased on a daily basis. Apart from bread and drink, most of the daily accounts consist of little more than large quantities of beef, mutton, and chicken.

Little information is given as to the preparation of meat. In wealthy Scottish households, large joints of fresh meat were usually roasted over the open fire on spits. The meat would then be served hot and the cold remains produced at a

[6] A. Gibson and T. Christopher Smout, 'From Meat to Meal: changes in diet in Scotland', in *Food, Diet and Economic Change Past and Present*, ed. by Catherine Geissler and Derek J. Oddy (Leicester and London, 1993), pp. 10-34.

Timothy Ross, ruins of Douglas Castle, c.1880. Douglas Castle near Lanark, the ancestral home of the Earl of Angus, was several hours' ride away from Glasgow.
National Library of Scotland, MS.707, no.4.

Cauldrons have changed little over the years. Cooking vessels similar to these would have been used by the Earl of Angus's servants in 1608. National Museums of Scotland.

later meal. Flesh of an inferior quality was placed in a large cauldron suspended over the fire and cooked slowly in a liquid with barley and vegetables. If a sizeable piece of meat remained after cooking, it would be removed from the cauldron and served on a platter as 'sodden' beef. The liquid left behind provided a nutritious soup, sometimes enriched with pieces of meat and prunes.

There was no shortage of fresh meat on the Earl's table. Given that the accounts cover the months from June to November, this is to be expected of an aristocratic family. Although constrained, they had plentiful supplies of money for their daily requirements, and access to cattle and sheep from their estates. Had the household accounts for the winter and spring survived, the story might have been very different.

After the summer's grazing, domestic cattle were at their peak. Winter fodder was expensive, and it made sense for farmers to kill a large proportion of their herd and preserve the flesh against the coming winter months.[7] William Ellis wrote of Scotland in the 1720s that the shortage of mutton and beef was so great that, 'at or about Martinmas, such of the inhabitants who are anything beforehand with the world salt up a quantity of beef, as if they were going on a voyage'.[8] This practice was general in Scotland until at least the late eighteenth century, when improved methods of agriculture and the introduction of new crops of potatoes and turnips made the provision of winter fodder for most animals feasible.

Over the centuries, various methods of preserving fresh food have been adopted, the most common being pickling, drying, salting, smoking, canning, and freezing. Of these methods, the first four had been in use for centuries by the time of the Earl of Angus's sojourn in Glasgow; canning and freezing were yet to be developed. Steeping in strong solutions of salt to prevent bacterial growth, and pickling in vinegar were both used by the Earl's servants.

In the accounts, salt was bought by the peck—a measure of capacity for dry goods equivalent to almost two imperial gallons. Half a peck of salt usually lasted

William Brownrigg, Common Salt *(London, 1748).* *National Library of Scotland.*

[7] For a detailed discussion of food preservation, see *Waste Not Want Not: Food Preservation from Early Times to the Present Day*, ed. by C. Anne Wilson (Edinburgh, 1991).

[8] William Ellis, *Country Housewife's Family Companion* (London, 1750), pp. 69-70.

a fortnight. From time to time, much greater quantities were bought in, indicating larger-scale activities. Vital for the preservation of a wide range of foodstuffs in the days before refrigeration, high-quality salt was produced commercially from the salt-pans of France, Spain and Portugal. In practice, due to the vagaries of war and the weather, it was frequently unavailable in distant Scotland. When it could be had, foreign salt was often prohibitively expensive.

The solution found by the resourceful Scots was to produce their own, albeit inferior, salt. Many coastal households made salt for domestic purposes by boiling sea-water in kettles on the hearth. However, from at least the late sixteenth century, most Scots preferred to buy commercially produced salt. In the 1630s, Sir William Brereton, an English visitor to Scotland, commented on the 'innumerable' salt-works on the east coast of the country.

The most important salt-producing area in Scotland was along the Forth estuary, particularly its southern shore from Musselburgh to Prestonpans.[9] Further north, a string of salt-pans stretched from the city of Dundee to Brora in Sutherland. Another concentration, along the coasts of Ayrshire and Dumfriesshire, emerged in the south-west. Salt was also worked in the Hebrides to such an extent that on his Highland tour with Dr Johnson, Boswell noted that the chief exports of the island of Iona were iron and salt.

In an age hindered by poor communications and transport facilities, where a household bought its salt depended largely on geography. As the largest centre of population, Edinburgh was an important market. Much of the salt coming into the city was carried on the backs of doughty 'saut-wives' from the pans at Joppa and Pinkie. Larger-scale trade involved merchants from as far away as Glasgow. Much of the salt they dealt in was transported to its market by coastal boats.

Anxious to protect their livelihood, the salt-producers, and the merchants who bought and sold their wares, were responsible for the insistence of the Scottish Parliament in the 1660s that only salt made in Scotland should be used for domestic purposes. After the Act of Union of 1707 they ensured that their favoured status continued by negotiating lower taxes for Scottish salt than for imported salt. When the salt taxes were repealed in 1823, their protected status was stripped away and Scots were able to purchase the better quality European 'Bay salt' (from the Bay of Biscay) and Cheshire rock-salt without discrimination.

Once salted, beef would keep for months, but in order to make it edible the meat had to be boiled for hours. Alternatively, it could be placed in a broth with large quantities of vegetables and barley to take up the salt. The combination of the poor quality of home-produced salt, the expense of the imported product, together with the effort involved, meant that salt as a preservative had its disadvantages.

The Earl of Angus's servants also pickled meat. A chopin (equivalent to two imperial pints) of vinegar costing four pence was bought at least twice a week. Pickling, the boiling of flesh in an acid solution, had been known for centuries, but became increasingly popular from the sixteenth century.[10] The most common

[9] Christopher A. Whately, *The Scottish Salt Industry, 1570-1850: An Economic and Social History* (Aberdeen, 1987), pp. 3-6.

[10] Jennifer Stead, 'Necessities and Luxuries: Food Preservation from the Elizabethan to the Georgian Era', in *Waste Not Want Not*, pp. 81-4.

pickling solutions were vinegar, made from sour wine, alegar from sour ale, and verjuice made from the juice of unripe crab-apples, all of which were considerably milder than modern vinegars. Giving the best flavour, wine vinegar was preferred by the wealthy. Pickled meat tasted better than salted meat; it was also cheaper and more convenient.

Beef and mutton often arrived in larger quantities than the family could eat before putrefaction set in and so had to be preserved. However, poultry was either bought on a daily basis, or taken from the Earl's hen-house, as required. Accordingly, it might be expected that fewer chicken dishes would be served. This is not the case, and poultry in one form or another appears almost daily in the accounts.

Chickens and capons at two shillings and sixpence each were standard fare for the family. As with beef and mutton, these birds were either roasted whole, or cooked in the soup. When there were visitors, a much greater variety of fowl was served. Geese, grouse, moorfowl, partridges, plovers, and larks all appear in the accounts on these occasions. Even in the summer, game was expensive: in June, partridges cost eight shillings each. In November, when Lord Hume came to dinner, the price had risen to the extent that two pairs of plovers and a partridge cost a total of forty-five shillings.

As a devout Roman Catholic, the Earl of Douglas did not eat meat on Fridays. Typically, the family's diet on non-meat days consisted of fish, both fresh and salted, together with large quantities of eggs, bread, and milk. On Friday, 22 July 1608, 'twa fresche salmond xvsh ane half hunderd fresche hereing xvish viiid fowr dosoun aiges [eggs] vish thre poynts milk iiiish fowr pound plowdames [plums] xiish' were taken from the larder. All the fish were eaten.

The accounts show that a considerable variety of fish was available. In addition to the salmon and herring, on non-meat days the family ate trout, whiting, and oysters. Very little fish was eaten except on these designated days. After the Earl of Angus's family had left Glasgow for Edinburgh, their accounts show a noticeable increase in the amount of fish purchased. Edinburgh being a coastal city, it is hardly surprising that fish, a highly perishable commodity, was more readily available there than in inland Glasgow.

Salt fish, such as 'cowtis dry keling' (a large dried cod), salt salmon and herring, supplemented the supply of fresh fish. Overall, but especially in the Glasgow accounts, they make up a substantial proportion of the fish eaten by the family. Dry salt fish, particularly salmon, was important in the trading economy of medieval Scotland both in the internal and export markets: from at least the thirteenth century, large quantities of salted salmon were exported from Aberdeen to the Continent. These fish would have been hard, dry, and extremely salty. By the early seventeenth century, even though dried salt fish kept better, they were fast losing popularity in favour of wet salt fish, such as herrings or oysters packed in barrels of brine.

The medieval tradition of observing fish days was declining in Scotland. This trend is illustrated by the surviving records of eating habits at Scotland's universities.[11] The diet books of St Leonard's College at St Andrews University for the

[11] A. Gibson and T. Christopher Smout, 'Food and Hierarchy in Scotland', in *Perspectives in Scottish Social History*, ed. by Leah Leneman (Aberdeen, 1988), pp. 39-43.

late sixteenth century show a rigorous observation of fish days, as do those of Glasgow University for 1602. There, masters and students breakfasted on eggs, bread, and ale. Dinner and supper consisted of soup, eggs, three fish dishes, bread, and drink. By the 1640s, there had been a pronounced change. Fish was still eaten, although not in great quantities, but it was now served alongside meat, and not reserved for formal fish days.

Many early accounts of visitors to Scotland claimed that the Scots did not eat vegetables.[12] While the Earl of Angus's accounts do not bear this out entirely, it is fair to say that vegetables were not of great importance in the family's diet. Herbs of one sort or another are the only green-stuff bought with any regularity. Otherwise, cabbages and parsley came in June, 'bownsches of sybus' (bunches of spring onions) in July, carrots in September and cabbages in October. Most of these vegetables were probably intended for the broth.

If vegetables are of scant importance in the accounts, then fresh fruit is almost entirely absent. The sum of references amounts to a single purchase of gooseberries. Perhaps the family had a source of home-grown fruit, such as apples and pears, and so did not need to buy fruit. Possibly the absence of fruit from the accounts is due to fear and suspicion. In the Middle Ages and beyond, fresh fruit was often blamed for the illnesses and even deaths brought on by seasonal over-indulgence. So great was the fear that in England the sale of fruit in the streets was forbidden in 1569. The result was that, apart from the likes of wild berries, fruit was generally unknown to most people.

The accounts note frequent purchases of expensive imported dried fruit. Prunes, in particular, were bought regularly. A 'quarter hundred plowdmss [prunes]' cost six shillings. One early visitor to Scotland recorded his horror at being faced with a dish of soup swimming with lumps of meat and prunes.[13] A pound each of figs and raisins at a total cost of twelve shillings were bought almost once a week, probably for this purpose.

Almost without fail, the first entry in the accounts each day was for the family's daily supply of bread. Of great importance in the diet, bread provided much needed bulk and roughage. In early sixteenth-century Scotland several different varieties of bread were available.[14] Of these, the Earl bought only two: menschotts (manchet), and much smaller quantities of the cheaper 'aitt bred' (oat bread).

Manchet, the menschotts of the accounts, was a favourite. The most expensive bread available, these small loaves of white bread cost as much as a shilling each. Even at this price, the family regularly consumed as many as fifty a day. As a dozen eggs could be bought for one shilling and sixpence, manchet was only eaten by those who could afford to be fastidious. A light and well-seasoned bread, the best manchet was unleavened and whitened with egg whites.

While the Earl of Angus's servants could satisfactorily roast meat on spits, and boil a wide range of meat, fish, and poultry in cauldrons suspended over the open fire, they had no oven, and so had to pay someone else to cook their baked dishes. Sometimes, they bought meal which was then given to a baker to make bread for the household. More often, the family simply bought the finished product.

[12] P. Hume Brown, *Early Travellers in Scotland* (Edinburgh, 1891).

[13] *Early Travellers in Scotland*, p. 88.

[14] F. Marion McNeill, *The Scots Kitchen* (London and Glasgow, 1929), p. 178.

In addition to bread, bakers produced a range of baked goods. So, the accounts record the expenditure of the not inconsiderable sum of eight shillings 'for bakeing of four pastries'. Once, shortbread is bought from a baker, and on another occasion the flour to make it was supplied to him.

Wheaten bread as bought by the Earl of Angus was a mark of status. The vast majority of the population had to content themselves with oat bread. Due to the climate and methods of cultivation employed, compared with England, relatively little wheat was grown in Scotland before the effects of the agricultural improvements and better communications of the eighteenth century were felt.

Oats, the staple food of Scots for centuries, have featured in accounts of the Scottish diet at least from the time of Jean Froissart, the fourteenth-century French chronicler.[15] Froissart wrote that Scots soldiers existed on a diet of 'flesh, half sodden, without bread'. Behind his saddle, each soldier carried a metal plate and a bag of oatmeal which was produced when he had eaten his fill of meat. The plate was then heated over the fire, and the oatmeal, mixed with water and shaped into cakes, was cooked on the plate 'like a cracknel or biscuit'. Oatcakes were made in much the same manner, cooked on a girdle at the domestic hearth, perhaps with the addition of a little fat.

As with bread, drink was bought in for the Earl of Angus and his household on a daily basis. Ale was the everyday beverage for the majority of Scots, accompanying each meal, including breakfast, until at least the early nineteenth century. Most households brewed their own ale. The Angus family bought in their ale presumably because they were living in lodgings and unable to brew their own. Some of their ale was bought from Mrs John Ross, the landlord's wife. As a rule, most small-scale brewers tended to be females. These women made more than was necessary for their own family's consumption and sold the surplus. Small beer, bought for the 'bairns', cost less than a shilling a gallon, but stronger ale at twelve shillings a gallon was also available. Just as with the bread for the household, sometimes the Earl and sometimes the brewer provided the ingredients.

The Earl of Angus also had a taste for wine. Purchased daily in quantities of two or three pints, wine was served at most meals.[16] Most of the wine drunk by the Douglas household was French, but now and then, particularly when guests were present, a chopin of Spanish wine, Malaga, Canary, Sack, or 'Candie wine'[17] was served. Purchases of 'aquavitie' (aquavitae) came from the same source as the wine. Possibly the Earl had acquired a fondness for wine during the years he spent in France. However, he was not alone in enjoying a glass of claret, as wine from the Continent was imported to Scotland from at least the late thirteenth century.[18]

Unfortunately, the accounts do not stipulate who, among the family and servants in the house, drank wine and who drank beer. It is known from other ac-

The Galloway Mazer, 1569.
Vessels such as the Galloway Mazer were used by the Scottish nobility for drinking wine. *National Museums of Scotland.*

[15] *Early Travellers in Scotland*, pp. 8-9.

[16] A Scots pint was three times the quantity of an English pint.

[17] 'Candie wine' probably means Cretan wine. Crete acquired the name Candia or Candy because of the sugar grown there. Wine from Crete was imported to Western Europe in the late Middle Ages.

[18] Billy Kay and Cailean Maclean, *Knee Deep in Claret: A Celebration of Wine and Scotland* (Edinburgh, 1983), p. 8.

Tantallon Castle, The Douglas stronghold in East Lothian, from William Daniell, A Voyage Round Great Britain *(London, 1814). National Library of Scotland, in MS.6140.*

counts of this period that the privilege of drinking wine was given only to those of the highest rank. The household arrangements for James VI on his marriage to Anne of Denmark in 1589 make it clear that wine was not permitted below the rank of the most important courtiers.[19] Wine was the drink of the nobility, not of the common man.

The arrival of visitors inevitably necessitated increased quantities of food and wine. Visitors also occasioned a greater variety and better quality of foodstuffs. When Lord Wedderburn, Lord Hume, Lord and Lady Douglas, and Lady Broughton came to visit on 3 November 1608, geese, rabbits, partridges, and plovers were served as well as the usual beef, mutton, and chicken.

While today partridges and plovers are still delicacies, then rabbits too were a luxury. Rabbits are not native to Scotland, having been imported by the Normans. Generally, only on estates with warrens looked after by a warrender did Scots eat rabbit. In the Earl of Angus's household, they were served only 'when sundry friends and gentilmen dynit', and cost ten shillings each against the two shillings and sixpence paid for chickens. Alexander Johnston, visiting from Tantallon, brought two pairs as a present. Then as now luxury foods made an acceptable gift.

The visitors of 27 June 1608 were perhaps not quite so welcome as the Earl's family and friends, but were still accorded hospitality. This delegation of clergymen intent on persuading the Earl to renounce his faith was a sizeable visitation

---

[19] J.T. Gibson Craig, 'Papers Relative to the Marriage of King James the Sixth of Scotland with the Princess Anna of Denmark, 1589', *Bannatyne Club*, 26 (1828), pp. 3-38.

which included some of the most important ministers in the west of Scotland. Among them were the Bishops of Glasgow and Galloway, the Provost of Glasgow, and the Commissioner of Glasgow. Their discussions with the Earl of Angus must have been prolonged, as they stayed for both dinner and supper.

On the table that day there was the usual fare of menschotts and oat bread, beef steaks, roast mutton, chickens, and eggs. In addition, provisions bought included a tongue, five moorfowl and their pullets, 'ane suckein weall' (a suckling calf), skink (a soup made from shin of beef), prunes, herbs, sugar and olive oil. To drink there was French wine, Malaga wine and beer.

One of the purchases listed for the visitors was a 'half pound of canerie succor xviiish iiiid', that is, sugar from the Canary Islands. The only other time that sugar is mentioned a full pound was bought. Before about 1650, fruit, berries, and honey were the major sources of sweetness in Britain, and even they probably did not feature significantly in the diet. Only the richest members of society were able to afford sugar.

Sugar made from the juice of the cane had been introduced to Europe by at least 1100 AD. First, it came as an import from the Middle East, Persia, and India. Later, with the Arab conquest of Southern Europe, sugar-cane was cultivated in Sicily, Cyprus and Malta.[20] Throughout the Middle Ages, sugar was grouped with other rare and expensive imports such as spices, including pepper, nutmeg, mace, and ginger.

Available only to the wealthy, sugar had many uses. In Roman times, it had been known only as a medicine, and undoubtedly this remained one of its main functions. However, in the Middle Ages sugar was used by monarchs and their most important nobles as a means of displaying status, wealth and power. When mixed with substances such as oil, water, gum, or ground nuts, sugar could be transformed into a pliable solid which could be moulded and decorated. Sugar figures produced in this way formed centre-pieces for the dining tables at court and in great houses. Although these figures were intended to be eaten, their principal role was to impress guests with the host's rank and wealth.[21]

Given his distressed state and the small quantities involved, the sugar purchased for the Earl of Angus is unlikely to have been used in such an extravagant way. He probably bought sugar primarily for its medicinal qualities, but may also have treated it in much the same way as spices, using small quantities as a condiment. As such, sugar was added to alter the flavour of food rather than to sweeten it.

Small quantities of other expensive imports were bought infrequently, including pepper, saffron, ginger, and on one occasion an ounce of cloves. Half a pound of ginger cost twelve shillings. Spices from the East are recorded in Egypt as early as 1450 BC. From the earliest days, the spice trade from distant Malaya, Indonesia, and China was controlled by the strategically placed Arabs. Travelling thousands of miles across dangerous seas and alien territories, the spice caravans were away for years at a time in pursuit of their quarry. Not surprisingly, the price of spice was high. The Arabs' monopoly of the trade was broken only in the first century AD when consumption of spices by the Romans reached a level the Arabs were unable to meet.

[20] Sidney W. Mintz, *Sweetness and Power: The Place of Sugar in Modern History* (London, 1986), p. 24.
[21] Mintz, p. 79.

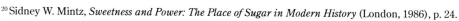

When and how spices reached Scotland is uncertain. Roman food, certainly, was heavily spiced, and it seems that the Romans brought spices with them when they came to Britain. How far their cookery was adopted by the native Britons is again largely speculation, but the use of spices declined after the Romans retreated to their homelands. Interest in spices was revived in the early Middle Ages, and returning Crusaders may have come back with an acquired taste for highly spiced food. This time the Venetians controlled the lucrative trade between East and West.

Having a variety of uses, spices were an extremely valuable commodity in both the culinary and medicinal worlds. In cooking, they were used in small quantities as condiments, and also played an invaluable role in disguising the taste of putrefying food. As with sugar, the purchase of spices had important symbolic overtones: as luxury goods, their use denoted the wealth and status of the household.

Familiarity did not alter William Douglas's negative feelings towards Glasgow, and in August 1608 he wrote again to the King, requesting that he and his family be allowed to go abroad. This time the King granted his wish, issuing a warrant permitting him to leave for the Continent before 10 November of that year. According to the household accounts, the family left Glasgow on 18 October 1608. Thereafter there are no entries until 25 October, when they reached Edinburgh.

The family's itinerary between leaving Glasgow and arriving in Edinburgh is unknown. Probably some time was spent at Douglas Castle making arrangements for their departure from the country and taking leave of family and friends. The Earl may also have spent time en route at a roadside inn. Surviving accounts of visits to Scottish inns tell a sorry tale of inedible food and a generally inhospitable welcome.[22] Not all of these reports should be taken at face value. Many were written by travellers ill-disposed towards Scotland who set out to shock their English readers with stories of the barbarous conditions prevailing across the Border.

Unfortunately, no innkeeper's bill for the Earl of Angus has survived. However, seventeenth-century bills for meals served to another Scottish aristocrat, the Earl of Tweeddale, while travelling on business between Yester in the Scottish Borders and London do exist. They may say nothing of the welcome given to the travellers, but the food served was perfectly adequate, comparing favourably with that eaten by the Earl of Angus in his lodgings.

In October 1667 the Earl of Tweeddale, accompanied by at least twelve others, made the journey from Yester to Durham and then on to London. His accounts include £22 8s 'to your Lo[rdship's] super [supper] and breakfast at Kelso'. The bill itself details a prodigious supper of broth, mutton, 'cold beif wt carits [carrots]', roast mutton, roast beef, chicken, bread, pears, and apples, all washed down with wine. Breakfast the next morning consisted of '2 dish milk and breid', '2 dish of Soups wt Collops [chops]', '2 peic beef', bread, wine and ale.[23] Whatever the quality of the fare served, in quantity it was certainly substantial. The Earl of Yester and his party would not have gone hungry.

Once the family was established in Edinburgh, the final weeks of the Earl of Angus's accounts reveal a good deal of coming and going between their Edinburgh home and Tantallon Castle. The accounts close on 19 November 1608,

[22] *Early Travellers in Scotland.*

[23] National Library of Scotland, Yester papers, MS.14628, ff.8, 122.

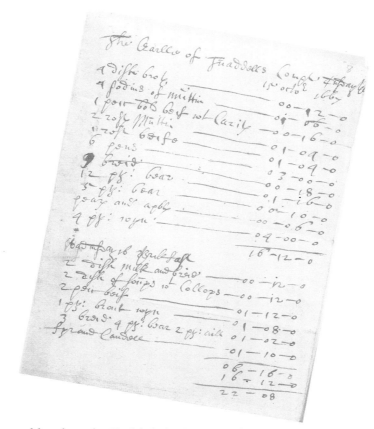

Innkeeper's bill for the Earl of Tweeddale, Kelso, 1667.
In October 1667, the Earl of Tweeddale and his retinue spent a night at a Kelso inn while travelling between Yester and London. Their supper included cold beef and carrots, mutton, chicken, pears and apples.
National Library of Scotland, MS.14628, f.8.

J. Bouillart, Histoire de L'Abbaye Royale de Saint Germain des Prés *(Paris, 1724).*
Forbidden to return home to say 'a last gudnicht' to his family, the Earl of Angus died in Paris in 1611. His tomb lies in the Abbey Church of St Germain des Prés. *National Library of Scotland.*

presumably when the Earl left for France. In 1609, the ailing William Douglas made a final petition to James VI and I for permission to return to Scotland to say a 'last gudnicht' to his family. The King refused and Douglas died in Paris in 1611.

Few Scottish household accounts survive as early as those of the Earl of Angus.[24] Hounded for his religious beliefs for decades, the Earl still had considerable means, being able to afford the best white bread available and to drink wine on a daily basis. When the need arose, he could afford delicacies such as partridge and plover out of season. There is little to suggest that the Earl tried to reproduce in his Glasgow lodgings the made-up dishes and sauces which he had experienced at the French court. The accounts do have their limitations (particularly concerning the number of mouths fed), but they show that the family ate in considerable style as befitted their status.

Much of the importance of the accounts lies in the information they give as to the continued symbolism attached to food by the wealthy in the early seventeenth century. The seemingly extravagant lifestyle of this distressed aristocrat was not simply wasteful and ostentatious; rather, it served a very real purpose. In the medieval tradition, food did not simply provide nutrition: it also served to indicate the subtle gradations operating in this hierarchical society. In serving menschotts and wine in preference to the oat bread and ale of the common people, the Earl was effectively demonstrating his rank and power.

[24] Surviving household accounts include those for Mary of Guise, 1542-60 (Rosalind K. Marshall, 'The Queen's Table', in *Tools and Traditions: Studies in European Ethnography*, ed. by Hugh Cheape (Edinburgh, 1993), pp. 138-43), and the Duke of Lennox ('The Household Account of Ludovick Duke of Lennox . . . 1607', *Miscellany of the Maitland Club*, 1 (1840), 159-91).

2 MARMALADE, HAGGIS AND POTATOES

SUTHERLAND, 1683-1712

Bill of Robert Bruce, an Edinburgh goldsmith, to Katherine, Lady Doune, later Countess of Sutherland, 1702.
National Library of Scotland, Dep.313/504.
By permission of the Countess of Sutherland.

Three-pronged fork made by Robert Bruce, Goldsmith, Edinburgh, 1698.
National Museums of Scotland.

My Lady Doun her Accompt
To Robert Bruce Goldsmith

1702		lb	s	d
April 11	*To a turned snuf box wigh 1-8*	8	8	
	To a dozen of Pollished forks wigh			
	32-15 at 5 shill 4 pen per ounce	105	8	
	To a dozen of knife hafts wigh wigh			
	21-2 at ditto per ounce	67	12	
	To 4 salts wigh 14-3 at ditto per ounce	45	8	
	To the fashion of the forks	21	12	
	To the fashion of the salts	10	16	
	To the makeing the knife hafts	18		
	To the blades	7	4	

ON 21 NOVEMBER 1706, JOHN, 15TH EARL OF SUTHERLAND, PAID A BILL FOR £346 2s incurred by his late wife, Katherine Tollemache, then Lady Doune, to Robert Bruce, an Edinburgh goldsmith.[1] This significant sum purchased a dozen knives and forks, four salt-cellars, a turned snuff box, a pair of candle snuffers and a stand. The Earl and his Countess had a town house in Edinburgh, where the cutlery was bought. However, their home was Dunrobin Castle in Sutherland in the far north of Scotland, and it may be that these goods ultimately found their way there.

In medieval Britain, food, if not eaten with the fingers, was either speared on the end of a long pointed knife, or eaten off slices of bread called 'trenchers'.[2] In modern times, the use of forks was first recorded in eleventh-century Venice when the wife of the Doge shocked St Peter Damien by eating off a fork.[3] Forks gradually became more widespread, but even in Italy they were not commonplace for another two hundred years. In Britain, forks were known in the Middle Ages, but even great households often had only a single fork, usually reserved for eating sticky sweetmeats or serving meat. Forks as they are known today were brought to London in 1608 by Thomas Coryat. Even there, the use of forks by individual diners only became common after the Restoration in 1660. It was from this time that equal numbers of forks and knives began to appear on the dining tables of the wealthy. Forks probably reached Scotland through contacts with the London

[1] National Library of Scotland, Sutherland papers, Dep.313/555.

[2] From the French 'trancher' to slice. These slices of bread were used as plates, hence the term 'trencher man' to describe those who ate the bread as well as the food borne on it. This practice continues to this day in our habit of eating food spread on toast.

[3] Margaret Visser, *The Rituals of Dinner* (London, 1991), p. 189.

*'Dunrobin Castle,
Sutherlandshire', from
William Daniell,* A
Voyage Round Great
Britain *(London, 1814).
National Library of
Scotland, in MS.6140.*

court. The general acceptance of forks by the common people came centuries later.

Dunrobin Castle, the seat of the Earls of Sutherland, was described in 1628 by Sir Robert Gordon as 'A house well seated, upon and most hard by the sea, with faire orcheards'. There were 'pleasant gardens planted with all kynds of fruit, herbes, and floures, used in this kingdom, and aboundance of good Saphron, Tobacco, and Rosemarie'. He enthused, 'the fruit here is excellent, and cheiflie the peares and cherries'.[4] Despite its northerly situation, Dunrobin Castle had one of the earliest known gardens in Scotland.

Scotland before the Restoration has been portrayed as a 'cultural desert' as far as gardening is concerned.[5] According to this view, political instability, a hostile climate, and the defensive nature of baronial domestic architecture, did not encourage the planting of pleasure gardens, orchards, or kitchen gardens. This is clearly an over-simplification.

Vines grew in the monastery gardens of Montrose and Jedburgh in the thirteenth century at much the same time as the Priories of Pluscarden and Beauly in Morayshire were renowned for their fruit trees and orchards. Gardening expertise reached many Scottish monasteries through monks of Anglo-Norman origin who brought their skills north with them. As monasteries were required to be self-sufficient, it is to be expected that gardens would be attached to ecclesiastical houses. Generally, the monks were left to cultivate their plots in peace.

The Lord High Treasurer's accounts and the Exchequer Rolls show that the Scottish royal castles had gardens from at least the reign of David II in the fourteenth century. Pear and cherry trees were bought for the gardens of Edinburgh Castle (the latter from a monk at Culross in Fife). Onion, leek, and kail seeds were purchased for Stirling Castle.

[4] National Library of Scotland, Sutherland papers, Sir Robert Gordon, 'Genealogy and Pedigree of the Earls of Sutherland', Dep.314/2.

[5] E.H.M. Cox, *A History of Gardening in Scotland* (London, 1935).

In 1538, Mary of Guise, James V's second French queen, wrote to her friend, Mademoiselle de Tern, that while there were apples, plums, and pears to be had in Scotland, there was not the same range as was available in France. In her reply, the Queen's French corrrespondent confirmed that, as requested, she had despatched plum and pear trees of varieties previously unknown in Scotland.[6]

From the early seventeenth century, the style of domestic architecture in Scotland changed. Fortification was no longer of paramount importance, and in this climate the conditions favoured the emergence of a more carefree, frivolous lifestyle. Pleasure gardens, kitchen gardens, and orchards began to be seen as an indication of wealth and social standing, and were increasingly incorporated into the design of baronial houses.

One of the first recorded private gardens in Scotland is that at Seton in East Lothian. Sir Richard Maitland wrote in 1560, 'this Lord biggit ane grit dyk and wall of stane about the yarde and grit orcheart of Seytoun'.[7] In the mid-1630s, the garden at Seton included apple and other fruit trees. The gardener at Yester reported a harvest of 7,700 pears in 1662, and in the winter of 1681 to 1682 a large consignment of pear, apple, and plum trees of a wide range of varieties arrived from Pinkie in East Lothian.[8] Other early Scottish gardens are those at Edzell in Kincardineshire (laid out in 1604 by Sir David Lindsay), Drummond Castle, near Crieff, and Sir George Touris's garden at Ormiston in East Lothian.

To return to Sutherland, an anonymous, torn, somewhat dog-eared notebook among the Countess of Sutherland's archive bears out Sir Robert Gordon's claims for the garden at Dunrobin. Entitled 'Ane Book of Receipts May 3 :83 [1683]', the notebook consists almost entirely of recipes for fruit preservation: pippins, quinces, cherries, raspberries, oranges, lemons, currants, gooseberries, and plums are all mentioned.[9] There are instructions for 'past [paste] of pippin', 'the best way to preserve any sort of plumbs', 'for jilly [jelly] of courantes or gooseberries', and even for preserving oranges whole.

As most people felt that there were dangers in eating large quantities of fresh fruit, great importance was attached to fruit preservation. Hence, the cookery books of the wealthy tend to place a disproportionate emphasis on preserving, a task performed on relatively few days of the year, while they fail to note such everyday dishes as broth and roast beef.

The identity of the author of the Dunrobin recipe book of 1683 is unknown, but the hand and contents leave little doubt that the writer was female. From the early days of fruit gardens attached to private houses, the tasks of collecting fruit and preserving it to provide delicacies and sweetmeats for the cold winter months ahead fell largely to gently-born women.

Account of fruit trees sent to Yester from Pinkie, 1681.
In the winter of 1681 to 1682, pear, apple, and plum trees were sent to Yester from Pinkie House in Musselburgh. *National Library of Scotland, MS.14176, f.192.*

[6] National Library of Scotland, Adv.MS.29.2.4, no.45.

[7] John Fullarton, ed., 'Sir Richard Maitland's History of the House of Seytoun', *Maitland Club*, 1 (1829).

[8] National Library of Scotland, Yester papers, MSS.14714, f.1; 14716, f.192.

[9] National Library of Scotland, Sutherland papers, Dep.313/503.

Written in a single hand, the Dunrobin recipe book may have been the work of one of a number of female relatives of the Earl of Sutherland. The most likely author is the Earl's first wife, Helen, daughter of Lord Cochrane. She came to Dunrobin on her marriage in 1680. Whoever was its author, the recipe book shows a knowledge of a variety of methods of fruit preservation: boiling in syrup, jellies, pastes, and marmalades are all mentioned. A common factor of these recipes is sugar in large quantities.

The large-scale use of sugar as a sweetener and preservative came about only when social and economic conditions allowed for regular supplies at reasonable cost.[10] From about 1650, the emergence of the European colonies and the exploitation of the New World led to a vast increase in sugar production. As more sugar became available its price began to drop, and in less than a century sugar changed from a luxury item to a necessity for the privileged classes.

While sugar retained its earlier uses, as a condiment, decoration, and medicine, its culinary roles increased and diversified: it was added to many meat and fish dishes as a sweetener; used as a sweetener for puddings, and, later, hot drinks. In the Dunrobin recipe book, its role was as a preservative for fruit, both purchased and produced in the castle gardens.

Three of the twelve recipes in the Dunrobin cookery book are for marmalades.[11] The word marmalade derives from the Portuguese 'marmelo' meaning quince, and from the sixteenth to the eighteenth centuries marmalade on its own meant marmalade of quinces. Then, marmalade was generally a stiff preserve to which flavourings such as rosewater and ginger could be added. The quinces were boiled in water until soft, and then boiled again with their weight in sugar. Given the stiffness of the conserve, it tended to be poured into boxes rather than pots. When required, it was removed from the box and served in slices as a delicacy.

Marmalade probably first reached Britain as an import. Legend has it that Mary, Queen of Scots, took marmalade as a cure for sea-sickness. In this case, she must have brought it back with her when she returned to Scotland from France after the death of her first husband in 1561. Later in life, Mary is reputed to have asked for marmalade when taken ill at Jedburgh. From this episode comes the pun on her name, 'Marmelade pour Marie malade'. While the authenticity of these stories remains in doubt, over the years digestive and even aphrodisiac properties have been attributed to marmalade.

One of the recipes in the Dunrobin recipe book is for quince marmalade. This is unusual for Scottish recipe books, where quince rarely features, probably because of the difficulty of growing the fruit in such a northerly climate. However, a cookery book begun in Dumfries in 1722 gives a quince marmalade recipe incorporating the traditional link with Mary, Queen of Scots. This 'excellent marmalade which was given to Queen Mary as a New Year's Gift' consists of quinces, oranges, blanched almonds, preserved eringo root, musk, amber dissolved in rosewater, and small quantities of cinnamon, ginger, cloves, and mace.[12]

The principle of cooking fruit with sugar and then crushing it together was soon applied to other fruit. The resulting conserve resembled what we today know

[10] Mintz, p. 37.

[11] For a detailed discussion of marmalade, see C. Anne Wilson, *The Book of Marmalade* (London, 1985).

[12] National Library of Scotland, MS.10281, p. 327.

as jam. In the Dunrobin recipe book, these marmalades invariably had their names appended such as the 'marmalet of cherries' (set with the aid of redcurrants) and orange marmalade.

Yet more varieties of marmalade were known. Martha Lockhart, Lady Castlehill, includes marmalades of gooseberries and of wardens (pears) in her recipe book begun in 1711.[13] The Dumfries recipe book includes marmalades of apricots, plums, damsons, gooseberries, raspberries, oranges, lemons, and redcurrants, together with four for pippins.[14] These marmalades had a softer consistency than the quince conserve and were generally potted.

Alongside the legend connecting marmalade with Mary, Queen of Scots, is the tradition that Dundee is the home of orange marmalade. One morning in the early eighteenth century, a Spanish ship carrying a large cargo of Seville oranges was supposedly forced to put in at Dundee due to heavy winds. Her perishable cargo of oranges was offered for sale at low cost. James Keiller was unable to resist the bargain and purchased a considerable quantity. His ingenious wife, Janet, faced with the problem of what to do with the putrefying fruit, devised the recipe for what has been called, along with porridge, 'Scotland's chief gift to the breakfast table of the English-speaking world'.[15]

Given that the Englishwoman Rebecca Price copied her mother's instructions for 'marmalet of oranges' into her recipe book in 1581, the story of Janet Keiller cannot be the whole truth. Rather than inventing the conserve, what seems more likely is that James and Janet Keiller produced and sold orange marmalade on a larger scale than had previously been known. They can also be given credit for much of the popularity of shredded marmalade. The earliest orange marmalade recipes, such as that in use at Dunrobin, are for a beaten or smooth conserve in which the orange-peel and pulp were boiled until soft and then pounded in a mortar.

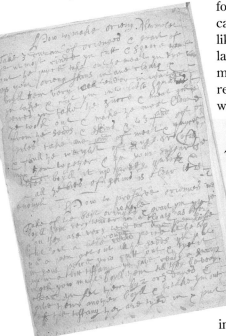

Recipe for orange marmalade 1683.
This small notebook, dated 1683, consists entirely of recipes for preserving fruit.
National Library of Scotland, Dep.313/503. By permission of the Countess of Sutherland.

How to make Orieng [orange] Marmolet

Take 3 duzan of orienges & grait [grate] of [off] ye utmost rinde yn cutt & squice [squeeze] out the juyce take out the meat yn tye up your orieng skins in ane cloath & boyll them very wel tender in water yn take & cut ym into litle Square peices yn take the succe [sugar] & meat qch [which] ye took out & make the meat Clean from the seads & skins & to 3 pnd [pounds] of piles take ane pnd of meat and juyce & full the weight of Suggar (of all) them together & qn [when] your suggar is melted boyll it up pretty quick & [?when] all the bitts of skins is clear it is enough.

In later recipes, such as that used by the Keillers, the orange-peel was cut into strips, producing shredded-peel orange marmalade. Pounding the peel in a mortar until smooth was a time-consuming task in the days before labour-saving devices, and dealing with large quantities of oranges as she was, it is understandable that Janet should look for shortcuts. In this case, perhaps there is some truth in the legend.

---

[13] *Lady Castlehill's Receipt Book: A Selection of 18th Century Scottish Fare*, ed. by Hamish Whyte (Glasgow, 1976), pp. 39-42.

[14] National Library of Scotland, MS.10281, pp. 324-36.

[15] McNeill, p. 235.

In addition to the recipe for orange marmalade, the Dunrobin notebook includes instructions as to 'how to preserve oranges whole'. Oranges had been imported into Scotland for the royal household from at least 1497 when the Lord High Treasurer paid three shillings 'for bering of the appil oreynzies [oranges] to the hous from the schip' at Leith and twelve pence 'for ane smal barel to send appillis oreynzeis to Falkland and Sanctandrois [St Andrews] to the King'.[16] As the Spanish ambassador was in Scotland at about the same time to negotiate a peace between James IV and Henry VII of England, he may have brought these oranges with him from Spain.

Soon, considerable quantities of oranges and lemons began arriving at the Scottish ports of Leith and Glasgow. Purchased by the gentry as well as the royal household, these were bitter Seville oranges. Oranges were put to several culinary uses: their juice was much sought after for flavouring sauces; orange-peel might be candied and eaten later as a sweetmeat or medicine or perhaps added to other dishes; as at Dunrobin, oranges were also preserved whole or made into marmalade.

In her manuscript, the author of the Dunrobin recipe book took no account of the daily provision of food for the table. Under the supervision of the Countess, the house steward was in charge of catering and domestic arrangements. One of the few servants' positions to survive from the Middle Ages, the house steward was usually of gentle birth, and one of the most important servants in an aristocratic household. His responsibility extended to all the food coming into the house, both those provisions which were bought in and those which arrived as payment for rent.

In the early 1700s, the house steward at Dunrobin was Hector Gray. His account book for March to November 1704 provides a detailed daily record of provisions coming into the house, and when and how they were used.[17] Most of the outgoings recorded are routine and are noted without comment. Being directly responsible to the lady of the house, Gray takes pains to note when he is acting specifically on orders from 'my lady'. So, on 25 September 1704, he writes, 'To the Boatmen who came from castle Stewart by my laddyes order . . . 2 firlots [of meal]'.

The lady of the house might be expected to be the Countess of Sutherland. However, for much of the time of the accounts, Earl John and Countess Katharine were resident in Edinburgh. Nowhere in the accounts is 'my lady' named: her identity would have been known to all at Dunrobin and so there was no need. This mysterious lady was probably the recently widowed Countess Jean Wemyss, mother of Earl John. She continued to live at Dunrobin after her husband's death in 1703.

The house steward also took orders from the chamberlain. Instructions from this important official are somewhat less frequent than those from 'my lady' but, when they do occur, are of much the same nature: 1 August 1704, 'To Johne Mathesone wright at the chamberland's desyre . . . 1 firlot [of meal]'. Supervision of the castle stores was a considerable responsibility, and the house steward was anxious to have a written record of all goods both incoming and outgoing.

[16] *Accounts of the Lord High Treasurer of Scotland, 1473-98*, ed. Thomas Dickson (Edinburgh, 1877), I, pp. 330-1.

[17] National Library of Scotland, Sutherland papers, Dep.313/551.

The first entries in Hector Gray's account book are for meal. The amount in store in the girnels (large chests or barrels for keeping meal) at the start of the accounting period is recorded, followed by the precise weight of meal delivered by individual tenants. The 'Discharge' then notes, 'what meal has been spent in the house of Dunrobin'. This is detailed down to the amount fed to the chickens and dogs, and that given 'to the woman who feeds the lambs'.

Similar records for oat, groats, beer (barley), and malt follow. The discharge for the latter takes the form of 'what malt has been brewen in the house of Dunrobin'. Ale was still very much the staple drink of Scotland. Living in the ancestral home, the household at Dunrobin was in a very different position from that of the Earl of Angus and his family in their Glasgow lodgings. As was more usual in great households, the ale for the Sutherland family was not bought in but was brewed on the premises, with the house steward responsible both for supplies of malt and the finished product.

Hector Gray's accounts make no mention of wine. Given the widespread use of wine by the aristocracy, it was undoubtedly served at Dunrobin, at least when the Earl was in residence. The explanation may well be that, as an expensive commodity purchased from a specialist supplier, charge of the wine was given to the chamberlain and not the house steward.

Sheep, kids, cattle, deer, fowl, and rabbits from the links are amongst the numerous live animals brought to Dunrobin as payment of rent in kind. Regular meat-eating, however, was not the norm in Scotland. As Dr Johnson wrote, most Scots 'seldom taste the flesh of land animals; for here there are no markets. What each man eats is from his own stock . . . no man can eat mutton but by killing a sheep'. Only the aristocracy ate meat on a regular basis.

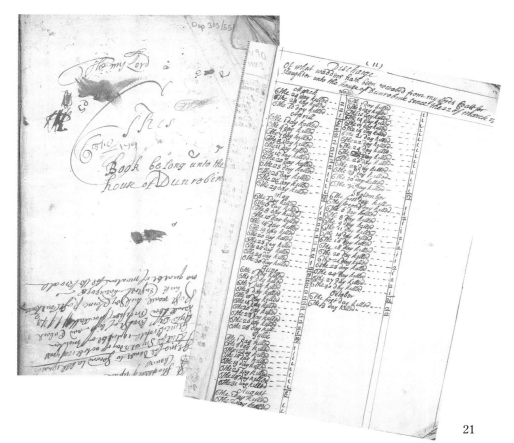

Account book of Hector Gray, house steward at Dunrobin, 1704.
Hector Gray's account book provides a daily record of foodstuffs received at Dunrobin and when and how they were used.
National Library of Scotland, Dep.313/551. By permission of the Countess of Sutherland.

By far the most numerous of the animals brought to Dunrobin were sheep: so numerous were they that separate records of incoming wedders, wathers and lambs were kept.[18] These were all animals received for slaughter. Killing took place regularly between March and October, with one or perhaps two animals slaughtered every second or third day, ensuring a plentiful supply of fresh meat for the table. Hector Gray's accounts take note of incoming supplies of salt. No doubt some of the meat would be salted down in readiness for the winter to come.

Between July and October 1704 no fewer than a hundred and twelve 'custome foulls' (fowl received as rents) were brought to Dunrobin. These must have been insufficient for the needs of the household, as there are numerous purchases of additional cocks, hens, and chickens. In April 1704 alone thirty-eight fowl were bought in. Chickens cost one shilling each, but cocks were one shilling and six-pence and hens two shillings. Some of the fowl were destined for long, slow cooking in the broth pot, and so size rather than tenderness was prized more highly than today. Others may have been bought for the hen-house to provide eggs for the table.

Sutherland being a coastal region, fishing was of great importance. Indeed, many of the Earl's tenants were fishermen. Large numbers of fish were received in lieu of rent, and accordingly Gray kept a record of 'what fish, hath been received from the Boatts'. In 1704, monthly totals of fish received ranged from 890 in April to 1,676 in May. These were probably mostly salmon, but Gray merely differentiates between great and small fish.

'Strathnaver, Sutherlandshire' from William Daniell, A Voyage Round Great Britain *(London, 1814). National Library of Scotland, in MS.6140.*

[18] Wedders and wathers are castrated male sheep.

Hector Gray's account book showing butter and cheese received at Dunrobin in 1704. National Library of Scotland, Dep.313/551. By permission of the Countess of Sutherland.

Although the majority of the entries are for flesh in one form or another, Hector Gray's records also cover other foodstuffs. In a typical week, the household consumed twelve dozen eggs at one shilling and sixpence per dozen. A pint of milk at one shilling and four pence was bought nearly every other day. On one occasion milk was bought 'for the collefours [cauliflowers]'. Even given that a Scots pint was equivalent to three imperial pints, a single pint cannot have gone far in such a large establishment. At this time, milk was not, of course, used in hot drinks, and its importance to children was as yet unknown. This may explain the low consumption. While milk was bought, other dairy products came in the form of rent. In June 1704, over ten stone of butter was received from two tenants. The same two tenants gave thirty-five stone of cheese in July and September of that year.

Cheese is reputed to have been made in Scotland as early as the thirteenth century.[19] Perhaps the best-known of the early Scottish cheeses is the oatmeal covered, buttery caboc. Tradition has it that this was made by Mariotta de Ile, daughter of a fifteenth-century Lord of the Isles. Cream and whole-milk cheeses ripened for three weeks or more, stored in ox-bladders, are also known. Another cheese, crowdie, made from skimmed milk, was similar to cottage cheese in con-

Dunrobin Diet Book, 1704-1712.
The Dunrobin Diet Book provides a glimpse inside the kitchen and dining room at the castle, giving detailed daily menus of the food served to the Earl of Sutherland, his family and servants. *National Library of Scotland, Dep.313/504. By permission of the Countess of Sutherland.*

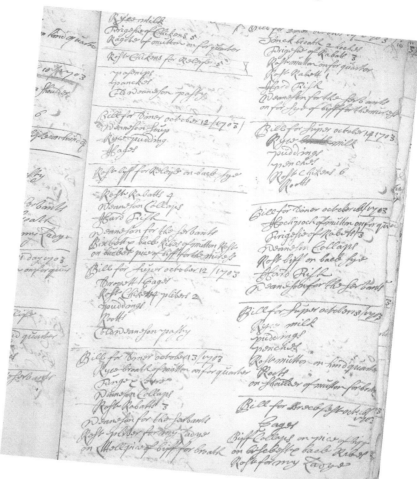

[19] Patrick Rance, *The Great British Cheese Book* (London, 1982).

sistency and texture. It may be this type of cheese that was made by the Earl of Sutherland's tenants.

Hector Gray's accounts provide a valuable record of the raw materials which formed the basis of the diet at Dunrobin. From the stores these foodstuffs were despatched to the kitchen. Details of how they appeared on the Earl's table are to be found in the Dunrobin Diet Book, also made up by the house steward.[20] Surviving for only the five months from 13 August 1703 to 26 January 1704 and for a short time in 1712, the Diet Book provides a glimpse inside the kitchen and dining room at Dunrobin, giving detailed daily menus of food served not only to the Earl and his family but also to his servants.

The Scottish gentry and aristocracy rose early, customarily going about their business for several hours before eating a hearty breakfast. This might consist of porridge, oat cakes and bannocks, bread, and possibly eggs, honey, or even soups, chops, and roast joints of meat. Few breakfasts are mentioned in the Diet Book. On the rare instances that they do occur, there is usually no mention of dinner: when the family was away from home for the day, breakfast became a more substantial meal served in its place.

Dinner was the most important meal of the day. In the sixteenth century, Mary Stuart ate at noon, but by 1704 the dinner hour for the nobility had been so far advanced that it had become fashionable to eat as late as two or three in the afternoon. Ordinary people still ate at twelve, while for others one was the preferred time. Then, as now, there was a distinction between meal-times in town and country: when in Edinburgh, the Earl of Sutherland probably ate his dinner far later than he did at Dunrobin.

Supper was another substantial meal. When dinner was late, supper was served between seven and eight in the evening. Much the same dishes appeared on the table at both meals. In the course of the eighteenth century, supper gradually became a lighter meal at which fewer joints of meat were served. In their place, rice and milk dishes, 'pochesh [poached] eggs' and a variety of delicacies appear. Supper was also the time for indulging in experiments with new dishes.

More often than not, the first item on the Dunrobin dinner menu was broth. The mainstay of much of Scottish cookery for centuries, broth consisted of meat or fowl cooked in a liquid, seasoned with garden herbs and vegetables and thickened with grains or oatmeal. The broth was cooked gently and slowly for several hours in a large cauldron hung over the kitchen fire. At Dunrobin, broth was based on beef, venison, hen, or mutton. Variations were 'skink', 'hoch poch' made with lamb or beef and flavoured with onions and carrots, game broth, or 'green soup', so called because of the addition of a seasonal green vegetable such as kail.

As one of the staple foods of Scotland known to all, there was no need to write down instructions for broth, and few recipes for soups and broths appear in early cookery books. This is especially so in the case of manuscript cookery books, usually intended only for the benefit of the author and possibly her family and friends. Writing in 1711, Lady Castlehill noted only one soup recipe, 'Artichoke Broth', made from globe artichokes.[21] It may well owe its inclusion to the unusual nature of the ingredients.

[20] National Library of Scotland, Sutherland papers, Dep.313/555.
[21] *Lady Castlehill's Receipt Book*, p. 10.

Bill for Diner october 15th 1703
Hoch poch of mutton on[e] for[e] qu[arter]
Frigesie of Rabets 3
Weaneson Collaps
Rost biff on[e] back syd[e]
Hard Fish
Weaneson for the Servants

Dunrobin Diet Book,
1704-1712.
National Library of
Scotland, Dep.313/504.
By permission of the
Countess of Sutherland.

On the table alongside the broth or 'hoch poch' were three or four meat dishes. As in the Angus household, much of the beef, veal, lamb, mutton, goat, and poultry was served roasted. 'Ro[a]st mutton on[e] for[e] quarter' and 'on[e] hind quarter of beefe' appear almost daily. There might also be a dish of boiled meat. In the case of beef, this was frequently accompanied by a vegetable, spinach, carrots, or cabbage being favourites. Rather less often, a dish of beef or mutton collops was served.

While most of the meat served at Dunrobin was from either cattle or sheep, the family also ate pork. In January 1704, roast pork was served on 12 January, boiled pork on the fifteenth and twenty-first of the month and later 'cold pig'. The house steward's accounts make no reference either to purchases of pigs or to pigs brought in by tenants in lieu of rent. A small number of pigs were probably kept at the castle in order to eat waste products and provide the occasional meal.

Traditionally, there has been considerable prejudice against pork in Scotland. This did not extend across the Border, and in Scotland, 'pork-eaters' was used as a term of contempt for the English.[22] Especially in the Highlands, pigs were thought unclean. Despite this, pigs were kept in significant numbers. Much of the meat from Scottish pigs, whether they were kept in Highland cottages or Edinburgh tenements, would be pickled and exported.

Game was served seasonally at Dunrobin, and then only rarely. Roast plovers, moorfowl, and wild fowl are the most common birds leaving the castle kitchen. From time to time, a roast hare or a 'Game Broath' is mentioned. Much more common are the pigeons from the doocot and the rabbits from the links brought in by the tenants. Treated as delicacies, as in the Earl of Angus's household in 1608, these animals were usually served roasted.

Joints of meat, too, were usually roasted or boiled, but new dishes in which pieces of meat were cooked in a sauce appear with surprising frequency. Chicken, rabbit, and to a lesser extent lamb and tripe, were served fricasseed, while 'rague [ragout] of veal', pigeons or chickens was increasingly popular. Fricassees and ragouts were two of a number of new dishes which effectively produced a more solid form of the ever-popular broth.

Lady Castlehill included a recipe for 'a Friggasy of Chickens' in her cookery book.[23] She called for the chickens to be half-boiled in good broth, skinned, and cut into small pieces. Chopped onions were then fried in hot butter to which were added the chicken pieces, anchovies, and some of the broth. The liquid was thick-

[22] Annette Hope, *A Caledonian Feast* (Edinburgh, 1987), p. 153.
[23] *Lady Castlehill's Receipt Book*, p. 32.

ened with egg yolks, and beaten with white wine and nutmeg, before being served with the addition of a few chopped capers. These new ragouts and fricassees clearly owed much to French cuisine.

Mary of Guise is often credited with introducing her native cookery to Scotland following her marriage in 1537. Certainly, there are accounts of lavish banquets and entertaining at James V's court, but there is no firm evidence of a change in cuisine. Indeed, Mary's influence at court lasted only about four years until James's death in 1542. Thereafter, her position was far from secure, and the tremendous interest in France and French culture was replaced by fear and suspicion.[24]

French cookery arrived in Scotland long before Mary's marriage.[25] Alexander II married Mary de Courcy of Picardy in 1239 and James I had a French cook. However, dynastic links with England can be traced back further, as Alexander I married a daughter of Henry I of England. What seems likely is that European, rather than purely French, cookery reached Scotland by two routes well before 1537: direct from France and indirectly via England. Scots travelling abroad, as scholars, soldiers, and merchants, as well as the much-publicised series of royal marriages, led to foreign influence on Scottish cookery.[26] Direct French influence on Scottish cookery was probably not of great significance until the late eighteenth century.

The harvest from the sea featured large in the diet of the inhabitants of Dunrobin Castle perched high above the North Sea. Fish appears on the table several times a week with no concession made to fast days. On most occasions fish is referred to either as 'hard' (dry salted) fish, fresh fish, or simply 'fish'. The 'hard' fish was probably ling and the 'fish' salmon. Cod's head, haddock and 'fryed perches' also appear. Sometimes the fish was served boiled. More often than not, no cooking method is specified.

Haggis, served as often as once a week at Dunrobin, may have been a favourite. By tradition, the word haggis was thought to come from the French 'hachis'; it is now thought more likely to derive from 'hag' meaning to hack or to chop.[27] Haggis consists of minced sheep's lights, liver, and heart, mixed together with oatmeal, suet, onions and spices, cooked and served in a sheep's stomach. F. Marian McNeill described haggis as 'a testimony to the national gift of making the most of small means'. This traditional Scottish dish provided a thrifty means of using parts of the animal which might otherwise be discarded.

Vegetables were rarely served with dinner, possibly because they were seen as a delicacy to be eaten in small quantities, and so not suitable for the main meal of the day. While meat dishes still dominated the table, vegetables appear on the supper menu as an accompaniment several times a week and were considerably more popular here than in the Angus household. Turnips and carrots were a favourite, 'earchokes' (artichokes) are also mentioned, as are parsnips and spinach and a new vegetable: potatoes.

[24] Rosalind K. Marshall, *Mary of Guise* (London, 1977).

[25] C. Anne Wilson, 'The French Connection Part II', *Petits Propos Culinaires*, 4 (1980), 8-20.

[26] Hope, *A Caledonian Feast*, p. 292.

[27] McNeill, p. 136.

In his famous *Herbal* published in 1597, John Gerard claims that potatoes originated in Virginia. From here evolved the tradition that Sir Walter Raleigh 'discovered' the vegetable there and subsequently introduced it to Britain. It is now recognised that potatoes originally came from Peru, and Raleigh's role in their transportation to Britain is uncertain. Certainly, Sir Francis Drake was aware of the value of the potato as a foodstuff as early as 1577. The confusion over their origin may have arisen because Drake took potatoes on board at Cartagena in Peru when en route to Virginia in 1586.[28]

By the early seventeenth century, potatoes had become popular in southern England at least to some extent on account of their supposed aphrodisiac properties. As early as 1604, Lady Elinor Fettiplace, of Appleton Manor in Berkshire, included buttered potato roots in her recipe book.[29] The new vegetable had reached northern England by 1673, when potatoes were grown as a garden crop at the Lancashire home of the Fell family in Ulverston.[30] In Scotland, references to potatoes appear from about the same time: according to Martin Martin they were eaten in the Hebrides in the 1690s;[31] in 1683, potatoes were grown in the garden of the School of Medicine in Edinburgh; and in the same year John Reid included them in his chapter on 'Fruit, Herbs and Roots for the Kitchen' in *The Scots Gard'ner*.

The earliest Scottish treatise on gardening, John Reid's *The Scots Gard'ner*, was first published in 1683. An experienced gardener, Reid had worked at Niddry Castle, Hamilton Castle and Drummond Castle. His book provides advice on the

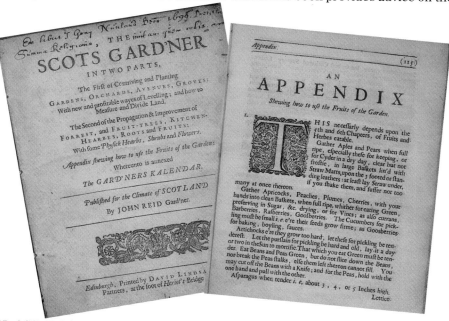

John Reid, The Scots Gard'ner *(Edinburgh, 1683).*
First published in 1683, *The Scots Gard'ner* is the earliest Scottish treatise on gardening. However, Reid also suggests methods of cooking garden produce.
National Library of Scotland.

[28] Redcliffe N. Salaman, *The History and Social Influence of the Potato* (Cambridge, 1949), p. 147.

[29] Hilary Spurling, *Elinor Fettiplace's Receipt Book* (London, 1986), p. 193. Lady Fettiplace probably used sweet potatoes imported from Spain.

[30] Helen Pollard, 'Lancashire's Heritage', in *Traditional Food East and West of the Pennines*, ed. by C. Anne Wilson (Edinburgh, 1988), p. 117-42 (p. 123).

[31] Martin Martin, *A Description of the Western Isles of Scotland c.1695, and a Late Voyage to St. Kilda. . .1698*, ed. by D.J. MacLeod (Stirling, 1934).

design and planting of gardens, and the particular problems of growing trees, flowers, fruit, and vegetables in Scotland. This is not simply a gardening book, as Reid suggests methods of cooking garden produce: in his own words, 'Showing how to use the Fruits of the Garden'. It is for this appendix to his book that *The Scots Gard'ner* has been dubbed the first Scottish cookery book.[32]

As with most vegetables, John Reid suggested a method of cooking potatoes. His advice was that they be treated in the same way as parsnips: 'boyl and peal [them], chop and bruise them well, powre on butter, and set them on a coal, and if you please strew a little cinamon upon them'. If no butter was available, sweet milk should be used instead.

The Sutherland Diet Book confirms that some of the wealthier members of society at least took John Reid's advice and experimented with potatoes in their gardens. However, as was the case throughout Britain, there was initially considerable resistance to the new vegetable, and it was to be some time before the full potential of the potato as a foodstuff for both humans and animals was realised.

While few desserts are mentioned in the accounts, those that do appear were invariably served at supper. Many of these desserts included garden produce. Gooseberry fool is mentioned in July and in the autumn there are stewed pears and apples. In the winter months an almond tart or a sweet pancake might appear on the table. Such dishes are few and far between. Like potatoes, desserts were considered novelties.

Usually, one menu was prepared for the family, but now and then individuals or groups required a separate meal. Sometimes, the children dined apart from the family, perhaps when meals were served too late for them to participate. Infrequently, separate menus were prepared for the Earl of Sutherland or for 'my lady'. More often than not, these meals comprised simply 'A dish of broth', suggesting indisposition. More substantial meals were prepared for George Gordon when he was expected home late after a day's work. His meals might consist of 'on[e] shoulder of weall [veal]', or a 'Littel pice of biff [beef]'.

As a matter of course, the servants ate from a separate menu. Although their diet was rather more monotonous than the food put before the family, they still ate well. Usually, just one dish is noted 'for the servants'. Typically they ate salmon, haddock, cold meat, and joints of roast venison. From time to time, cheese was served to the servants at Dunrobin, never to the family. Separate servants' menus were probably maintained as much to preserve social distinctions as for economic reasons.

The anonymous recipe book of 1683, together with Hector Gray's accounts and the Dunrobin Diet Book provide an insight into the eating habits of the Earl of Sutherland and his household. For such an important and privileged family, the meals served at Dunrobin were not notably extravagant. However, at the same time, although firmly based on traditional Scots cookery, the diet at Dunrobin was far removed from that of the Earl of Angus's household a century earlier.

New foodstuffs such as potatoes were known, more adventurous methods of cooking had become popular, as had sophisticated eating implements. With a

[32] John Reid, *The Scots Gard'ner* (Edinburgh, 1683). A modern edition of this work with an introduction by Annette Hope was published in 1988.

garden stocked with fruit, the family had the knowledge and the means to preserve it. After the Restoration of Charles II in 1660, English cookery became increasingly sophisticated. In time these new ideas were carried north by visitors to court. Although based in the remote north of Scotland, the Sutherland family was very much aware of current trends in Edinburgh and London, and were prepared actively to experiment with the food on their table.

3 SAUSAGES, TEA AND BARLEY

SALTOUN, 1688-1716

'FLORENTINE OF OYSTERS', 'ALMOND PUDDINGS', 'GOOSEBERRY CUSTARD' AND 'CAPON LARDED with lemon'. Written in her distinctive spiky hand, these recipes all appear in the cookery books of Katharine Bruce, Lady Saltoun. One of the two slim notebooks is inscribed simply 'Ka. Bruce, 1688', the other, entitled 'Dame Katharine Bruce's Book of Receipts', is undated.[1] In both volumes, Lady Saltoun uses her maiden name, as was the custom of Scottish women at the time. As Katharine was dead by 1715, both notebooks must predate the first Jacobite Rising.

Katharine Bruce was the daughter of Colonel Sir Henry Bruce of the Ordnance. After a childhood in Clackmannan, she married Sir Robert Fletcher of Innerpeffer in 1648. Some years prior to his marriage Sir Robert had sold the Innerpeffer estate near Dundee and purchased Saltoun from the debt-ridden 9th Lord Saltoun. Katharine's new home lay in the prosperous county of East Lothian, to the south-east of Edinburgh.

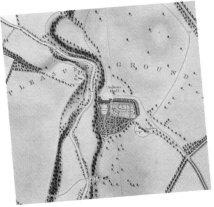

Detail from a 'Plan of the Estate of Saltoun', showing the area of Saltoun Hall, eighteenth century.
Saltoun in the prosperous county of East Lothian was purchased in the early 1640s by Katharine Bruce's husband, Sir Robert Fletcher.
National Library of Scotland, MS.17874 (22). By permission of J.T.T. Fletcher, of Saltoun.

Sir Peter Lely, 'Katharine Bruce, Lady Saltoun'. By permission of J.T.T. Fletcher, of Saltoun.

[1] National Library of Scotland, Fletcher of Saltoun papers, MSS.17854-5.

Unfortunately, Sir Robert died of consumption in 1665 at the early age of thirty-nine, leaving Katharine in her own words 'the most disconsolate widow'. A history of the family written in 1803 paints a most depressing picture: 'In a room hung with black, and lighted by the dead lustres, sat this Lady in her deepest funeral weeds'.[2] Katharine was to survive her husband by over forty years.

In spite of her obvious distress at the loss of her husband, Lady Saltoun found some consolation in her library. She was an educated woman, and her son, Andrew Fletcher, commonly known as 'the patriot' for his fervent opposition to the Act of Union of 1707, was to say of her 'if there is anything in my education or acquirements, during the early part of my life, I owe them entirely to that woman'.[3] Katharine's extensive library catalogue, which she called her 'Inventer [inventory] of my Bookes', extends to more than five pages of closely written text.[4] As might be expected for the time, most of the works are of a theological nature, but there are also books on British and European history, on literature and antiquities.

According to her library catalogue, Katharine Bruce did not possess any printed cookery books. This is perhaps not surprising. Although books on cookery had appeared in Europe from the fifteenth century – Italy produced Martino's *De honesta voluptate et valetudine* in 1474, and France Taillevent's *Le Viandier* in 1490 – they were usually aimed at court circles and consisted largely of special-occasion cookery for professional chefs.

Several recipe books were published in England during the seventeenth century. Among the earliest of these were the anonymous *A Closet for Ladies and Gentlemen*, of 1608; Gervase Markham's *The English Housewife*, of 1615; and *The Queen's Closet Opened*, of 1671. Until Robert May's *The Accomplisht Cook* of 1660, recipes tended to be included in general treatises on household management. Rather more practical than the French works, which elevated cookery to an art form, many of these English books were specifically aimed at gently-bred ladies, reflecting the rise in literacy among women. Mrs McLintock's *Receipts for Cookery and Pastry-Work*, the first recipe book published in Scotland, did not appear until 1736.[5]

One of Katharine Bruce's own manuscript recipe books is largely, but not exclusively (as in the case of the Dunrobin notebook), concerned with fruit preservation.[6] Raspberries, oranges, cherries, apricots, pippins, gooseberries, red and white currants, plums, and quinces are all mentioned. Of these, only apricots did not feature in the Dunrobin book. Much of this fruit was the produce of Katharine's own garden and orchard. The soil of East Lothian is exceptionally fertile, and to this day the area around Saltoun is famed for its market gardens and fruit farms.

Katharine notes two recipes for raspberry cakes and one each for orange and apricot cakes. These are not cakes as we know them today: rather, the fruit was

Gervase Markham, The Queen's Closet Opened *(London, 1671), one of a number of recipe books published in England in the seventeenth century. National Library of Scotland.*

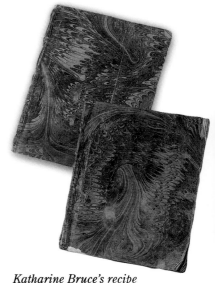

Katharine Bruce's recipe books. Katharine Bruce kept two recipe books. One is inscribed 'Ka. Bruce, 1688', the other is undated. *National Library of Scotland, MSS. 17854-5. By permission of J. T. T. Fletcher, of Saltoun.*

---

[2] Anon., *Recollections Respecting the Family of the Fletchers of Saltoun* (Edinburgh, 1803), p. 1.

[3] *Recollections*, p. 2.

[4] National Library of Scotland, Fletcher of Saltoun papers, MS.17861, ff.39-42.

[5] For a modern edition of this work, see *Mrs McLintock's Receipts for Cookery and Pastry-Work*, ed. by Iseabail MacLeod (Aberdeen, 1986).

[6] National Library of Scotland, Fletcher of Saltoun papers, MS.17855.

first cooked in water until tender, then sugar to the weight of the fruit was boiled to a candy with a little water. The fruit and sugar mixtures were then combined and poured onto flat dishes before being set 'in an oven for 2 or 3 dayes ... When they ar[e] dray [dry] put them owt'.

Jellies were Katharine's preferred method of preserving gooseberries, currants and pippins. Oranges were variously made into marmalades, jellies, paste or cakes, and quinces into jelly or marmalade, but her cherries were either bottled or dried. As part of the heraldic design of the Fletchers of Saltoun, cherries had a particular significance for the family.

TO PRESERVE CHIRIES

Tak the farest rip chirie [cherries] you can get tak away the stalkes and stones making as litell a holl as you can to every pound of chiries thus dresed tak 3 quarteres of a pound of fien shuder [sugar] & as mutch water as will melt it then put in the chiries & boill all together on a gasikelier faier skiming it softly till your sirop be strong & thik tak them af & lay your chiries as otheres sider in rowes in glasses with out any sirop & when your sirop is prity cold put on the sirop lat you chiries bee well covered with it & when they ar quite colld paper them up they will kip a year if you wolld have you chiries tast sharp boill a few red raspberries in the water you ar to dissolve your shugar in.

The second of Katharine's two notebooks is much more varied in its contents than the first, with recipes for poultry, vegetables, almonds, eggs, and shell-fish, as well as for fruit. This recipe book includes entries in another hand, that of Katharine's daughter-in-law, Margaret Carnegie. She also made some of the entries in the two other early eighteenth-century recipe books among the family papers.[7] Added to by successive generations, manuscript recipe books were intended as memory aids for family and staff, providing a repertoire of both new and tried-and-tested dishes.

Meat-based recipes are very much in the minority in Katharine's section of the notebook, suggesting that she adhered to old-fashioned roasting and boiling methods, rather than made-up dishes combining several ingredients. Mutton is not mentioned and beef is represented only by to 'Bak bif [beef] like venison'. There is also a recipe for pork sausages.

Sausages made from pig-flesh were known in Britain from at least Roman times. However, the prejudice that existed in Scotland against the pig has resulted in few recipes for pork dishes appearing in the nation's cookery books. Such recipes as do appear tend not to be regional dishes, but examples of an emerging British national cuisine. Sausages must have been quite a novelty at Saltoun.

Katharine's recipe for sausages called for tender, lean pork, cut into pieces and pounded in a mortar. To this was added fat, 'the leaf of the hog', the quantity being at the discretion of the cook 'as mutch as you think wid mak them fat a nuf [enough]'. The two were beaten together in the mortar until it comes 'a sunder with you fingeres & work like past'. Once the seasoning of cloves, mace, pepper, and salt, together with the grated bread was added, the sausages were ready to be put into their skins. English cookery books suggest twisting the sausages into

[7] National Library of Scotland, Fletcher of Saltoun papers, MSS.17856-7.

links as early as the 1630s, but no indication of this practice is given here. After light smoking in front of the fire, the sausages could be roasted on mutton or capons. In the days before refrigeration, perishability was a matter of great importance, and Katherine comments that prepared in this manner, the sausages 'will last good a wik [week]'.

TO MAKE SASEGES

Take the tendrest of the lean of fresh pork cut it in bites & beat it in a ston morter as fin as you can then tak of the leaf of the hog as mutch as you think wid mak them fat a nuf minglet & beat it well with the flesh in the morter when it is a nuf it will com a sunder with you fingeres & work like past then tak a litell grated bread seartch it with cloves mas [mace] pepper & salt & so work in this sesoning with your hand & so fill your skines thay most hang nier the faier they will last good a wik roast them upon muten [mutton] or capones theay ar very good.

Katharine gives three poultry recipes: 'How to boill chickenes', 'To boiell a Capon Larded with Lemon' and 'A Chicken Pay [pie]'. Pies were important for a number of reasons. Provided the case was completely air-tight, the food would remain edible for longer. In effect, the pastry case acted as a means of short-term food preservation.[8] Skins and bladders served the same purpose.

A strong pastry crust acted as a container in much the same way as a pottery or metal dish, rendering the food portable. These thick pastry crusts were sometimes considered more as containers than as an edible part of the dish.[9] Acting as containers for baking, transporting, and storing, as well as extending the shelf-life of the contents, it is hardly surprising that pies enjoyed considerable popularity.

A CHICKEN PAY

Cut your chickenes in halfes seson them with salt and peper nutmig ginger then lay them in the pay with bif marow sum curenes resines 3 or 4 dates a larg mas [mace] & so clos your pay & bak it in the mean time have a whit broth mad and whit wine or sak [sack] yolkes of egges shuger according to tast boill these together & put it in your pay when it is redy to come out of the oven and stro sum shuger upon your pay and serve it up.

Katharine Bruce's chicken pie has distinct medieval overtones as does much of her cookery, with the addition of large amounts of seasonings and flavourings: nutmeg, ginger, currants, raisins, dates, and sugar are all added, along with salt and pepper. Katharine specifies three or four dates, otherwise no quantities are given. Probably, only small amounts of each ingredient would be added.

After closing with the pastry lid, the pie was baked. Meanwhile, a white broth of white wine or sack (a dry white wine from Spain), yolks of eggs, and sugar was prepared. The lid of the cooked pie was removed and the sauce added. The lid was then replaced, and with a dusting of sugar, the pie was ready to be served.

---

[8] Peter Brears, 'Pots for Potting: English Pottery and its Role in Food Preservation in the Post Medieval Period', in *Waste Not, Want Not*, ed. by C. Anne Wilson (Edinburgh, 1989), pp. 32-65 (p. 32).

[9] Brears, p. 35.

This chicken pie was cooked in an oven. Only a few years later the family bought almond custards, gooseberry tarts, pigeon pies, seed bread, short bread, plum cake, and currant tarts from an Edinburgh baker.[10] However, the wording of Katharine's chicken pie recipe suggests that, unlike the Earl of Angus's household in 1608, the Fletchers had their own domestic oven.

The oven at Saltoun was probably no more than a cupboard set in the wall by the open hearth.[11] The more primitive ovens then in use were pre-heated by the insertion of hot embers from the fire which would be removed before the food was placed inside. More sophisticated ovens had double walls, the fuel being placed in the cavity between the two. Also available were Dutch ovens. These enclosed, free-standing, metal ovens had legs, a handle, and a hinged door. They could either be suspended over an open fire in much the same way as a cauldron, or they could be placed in the fire itself.

When a complicated meal was being cooked, the area over the fire could become extremely crowded, with saucepans and Dutch ovens in the embers, roast-

The hearth in the kitchen of the Georgian House, Edinburgh, c.1780. When a complicated meal was being cooked, the area over the fire could become extremely crowded. *National Trust for Scotland.*

ing spits suspended above the fire, and cauldrons and kettles on chains strung across the hearth. To add to this confusion, Katharine Bruce's cooking instructions for sausages specify that they 'must hang near the faier [fire]', presumably on hooks or chains.

Margaret Carnegie's recipes are generally more adventurous than those of her mother-in-law, being heavily orientated towards the new sauces. Mutton is represented by instructions for breaded cutlets in an anchovy and onion sauce flavoured with lemon juice and nutmeg. There are also 'Scotch collops' of sliced veal, floured and browned over a hot fire. They were served with forcemeat balls of minced veal and beef cooked in a ragout of bacon, mushrooms, and pickled cucumbers. Stewed pigeons, preferably tame, were 'soberly' simmered for an hour

[10] National Library of Scotland, Fletcher of Saltoun papers, MS.16855, f.72.

[11] For further information on early ovens, see Doreen Yarwood, *The British Kitchen: Housewifery since Roman Times* (London, 1981), pp. 80-1.

and a half in a sauce of claret, bacon, onions and spices thickened with breadcrumbs. For beef there is a recipe for 'A fine Pottage', and instructions as to how to stew beef.

In the latter case, the boned joint was salted, smeared with oysters, onions, grated bread and spices, and tied up in a cloth. It was then stewed in white wine and beef stock, together with yet more oysters, a pound of sausages, lemon juice, and butter. Finally, the dish was garnished with hard-boiled eggs and lemons.

The two fish recipes in the notebooks, 'To make a good Codes [cod] head' and 'To Dress pick [pike] or other such lyk [like] fish', the latter cooked in a claret and anchovy sauce, are both in Margaret Carnegie's hand. Given their proximity to the coast, it is likely that the family's diet included a good deal of fish. That no fish bills appear among the numerous tradesmen's accounts kept by the Fletchers at this time suggests that they bought their fish at the door from wandering tradesmen.

To Dres pick or such Lyk fish

Take a couple of pickes scraped them [sic] wash them clean then open them and save the blood then put them into a stew pan wt [with] a pint of watter a quart of claret & anchovise 2 onyons [onions], one of them stuft wt cloves a bunch of tyme [thyme] and a whole peper then put them altogether and let them stew soberly 3 quarters of ane houre then take a quarter of a pound of buter and burne it one the fire till it be black strow in a spoonful of flower then put this black butter into your sauce and let it stew a quarter of ane hour then dish it up and garnish your dish wt Lemon.

In the Middle Ages fish and meat were rarely mixed in the one dish. This distinction became blurred by the late seventeenth century. Oysters, in particular, were treated in a wide variety of ways. Popularly eaten on their own either fresh or pickled, they were also served in sauces, in pies, and, as in Margaret Carnegie's stewed beef recipe, increasingly as an accompaniment to meat and fish dishes.

Oysters have been eaten throughout the British Isles from at least Roman times. Along with partans (crabs) they were consumed in 1594 at the banquet in Stirling Castle to celebrate the baptism of Prince Henry, Charles I's unfortunate elder brother. In the eighteenth century, Edinburgh's oyster taverns, where revellers competed to consume the largest quantity of oysters, were notorious. Until overfishing made them a luxury in the twentieth century, oysters were both eaten to excess and used lavishly in cooking.

Katharine Bruce's 'Florentine of Oysters' called for parboiled oysters, white wine, a 'prity quantity of crummokes'[12] boiled, peeled, cut into pieces, all baked in a pastry case. In the beef stew the oysters were the accompaniment: here they are the main ingredient to which vegetables were added. In much the same way vegetables too could be either the principal or additional ingredient of a made-up dish.

Vegetables are mentioned frequently in the Saltoun recipe books, suggesting that their importance was increasing – an impression also given by the Dunrobin

---

[12] The crummoke or skirret was widely cultivated in eighteenth-century Europe. A root vegetable similar to the parsnip, it was generally eaten boiled with butter and pepper or blanched and then fried. Skirrets were also added to soups or meat dishes.

Diet Book. Boiled chickens are stuffed with 'parslay [parsley] in their bellies' and served in a sauce swimming in vegetables: crummokes or skirrets or 'boiled artichok botomes cut in quarters' are suggested.

Artichokes are accorded a recipe of their own. Boiled artichoke hearts were set in a dish on the fire with butter and sweet cream. To this was added bone marrow boiled with sliced ginger. The dish was then 'seasoned' with sugar and served with the popular 'conserve of barbaris' (berberries).

TO MAK A DISH WITH ARTICHOKES

Tak 6 artichokes boiell them tender tak onlly the botomes & lay them in a dish & set them on the faier with as mutch buter as thay will boill in when thay have boiled a wambell or two put in a quarter of a pint or mor of swit cream then tak marow & boiell with a litell slised ginger & when it is boieled a nuf put in your artichokes seson them well with shuger & so serve them up with conserve of barbaris.

John Reid may have encouraged Scots to grow their own vegetables in *The Scots Gard'ner*, but at Saltoun he was already preaching to the converted. As early as 1647, the Fletchers bought 'Seedis for the yaird of saltoun', growing their own lettuce, carrots, radishes, and onions amongst other vegetables.[13] From this time on, there are regular purchases of vegetable seeds, fruit trees, and gardening equipment.

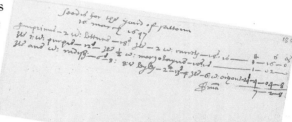

An early eighteenth-century gardener's diary gives some indication of the programme of work in the kitchen garden at Saltoun.[14] In January, spinach, radish, and carrots were sown in trenches, early salleting (celery), Windsor beans, and early peas were placed in a sheltered position, cauliflower and lettuce planted under glass, cabbages stored in a dry place, and turnips and parsnips transplanted. February was 'a busy month upon which depends much'. Directions are given to 'sow plenty' asparagus, onions and leeks, to plant potatoes, and transplant cauliflowers and artichokes if dry. In March asparagus, artichokes, carrots, cabbage, cauliflower, endive, and espaliers (fruit trees trained on a lattice) were planted.

Yet more activity was necessary to maintain the hotbeds (greenhouses). There, vegetables as varied as cucumbers, early peas, kidney beans, cauliflower, and asparagus were sown along with soft fruits from strawberries to melons. This carefully planned schedule provided the family with a steady and varied succession of fresh vegetables throughout the summer and autumn months.

Bread, butter, milk, cream, almond custards, seed bread, plum cake, and currant tarts were bought daily for the household at Saltoun both from local tradesmen and merchants in nearby Edinburgh. The minutiae of the family's purchases for over a century are recorded by the thousands of meticulously kept bills and

Above:
'To Mak a dish with Artichokes', Katharine Bruce's recipe book. Katharine Bruce gives a number of suggestions for cooking vegetables, among them this recipe for artichokes.
National Library of Scotland, MS.17854, f.4v. By permission of J.T.T. Fletcher, of Saltoun.

Right:
Bill for 'Seedis for the yaird of saltoun', 1647. In 1647, lettuce, carrot, onion and radish seeds were bought for the kitchen garden at Saltoun.
National Library of Scotland, MS.16852, f.180. By permission of J.T.T. Fletcher, of Saltoun.

[13] National Library of Scotland, Fletcher of Saltoun papers, MS.16852, f.180.

[14] National Library of Scotland, Fletcher of Saltoun papers, MS.17254, f.48.

receipts. These same vouchers reveal that from at least 1715 the Fletcher family was making regular purchases of a much more precious commodity: tea.

Tea was drunk in China for over a thousand years before it was brought to Europe in the mid-sixteenth century by Portuguese merchants trading in the East. Soon, the Dutch were carrying small quantities of tea to France and England, and it subsequently began to appear on sale in London. When the East India Company began importing tea to England in the mid-seventeenth century, distribution became more widespread, but many Scots must have first sampled the drink during visits to London.

Tradition has it that tea was introduced to Scotland by Mary of Modena when she accompanied her husband the Duke of York, later James VII and II, on his visit to Edinburgh in 1681. Firm evidence that hot beverages had reached Scotland is to be found in documentary sources such as Grisell Baillie's household inventory of 1696, which mentions 'a whit tee stop' and a 'coper pott' for coffee.[15]

On 31 May 1715, Margaret Carnegie settled a tradesman's bill for £33 16s 6d, including payment for 3lb of tea bought on four separate occasions.[16] Two types of tea, 'green tea' and 'bohea tea', were bought. Green or unfermented tea was the first tea drunk in Europe, while bohea or black tea only reached Britain towards the end of the seventeenth century. Although these were two of the cheaper types of tea, both were expensive compared with the cost of food at the time. Heavy taxation and high transportation costs meant that tea remained a luxury until the late eighteenth century when the existing tea taxes were repealed and replaced by a flat, lower rate.

In spite of the expense, tea, blended by the customer, quickly became the fashionable drink for ladies. The household's precious supply of tea was kept in a

'A Family at Tea',
Richard Collins, c.1720.
By courtesy of the Board
of Trustees of the Victoria
and Albert Museum.

[15] R. Scott Moncrieff, ed., 'Lady Grisell Baillie's Household Book, 1692-1733', *Scottish History Society*, Second Series 1 (Edinburgh, 1911), p. lviii.

[16] National Library of Scotland, MS.16854, f.106.

'Madam Fletcher's accompt for tea', 1715. Margaret Carnegie's bill for two and a half pounds of bohea tea and half a pound of green tea. *National Library of Scotland, MS.16854, f.106.*

special, often elaborate, tea caddy, the key to which was held by the lady of the house. In the wake of the new passion came the demand for table china. In order to drink tea in the accepted manner, the fashionable household must have a brass or copper tea kettle and a brass or porcelain tea service. At first, only imported china, usually from the East or Holland was suitable, but in the course of the eighteenth century English makers such as Chelsea, Derby, Worcester, and later Wedgwood met much of the demand. In its turn, the tea service had to be set out on a dainty tea table.

An 'Inventory of China' of about 1716 in the account book kept by Margaret Fletcher's son, Lord Milton, shows that the Fletcher family was no exception to this trend.[17] Their china collection was extensive. Along with the breakfast cups and saucers, soup bowls and ashets, there were four teapots and their respective sugar bowls and milk pots. Also, the inventory lists 'a doz blew and white Tea cups & sacers [saucers] from Holland', bought for two shillings and sixpence, together with numerous other cups and saucers, some of which were purchased in London. Elsewhere in the same account book is a note of eight shillings spent on 'a square wainscot Tea Table'.

Lord Milton's 'Inventar of China', c.1716. National Library of Scotland, MS.16933, f.16. By permission of J.T.T. Fletcher, of Saltoun.

[17] National Library of Scotland, Fletcher of Saltoun papers, MS.16933, f.16.

It was not to be Margaret Carnegie's propensity for tea-drinking but her business acumen which assured her place in history. While in exile in the Netherlands, Margaret's brother-in-law, Andrew Fletcher, had seen barley mills and fanners for winnowing corn. Recognising their potential for improving productivity on his own estate, he arranged for an East Lothian wheelwright, James Meikle, to visit Holland. There, he was 'to learn the perfect art of sheeling barley' and 'how to accommodate, order, and erect mills for that purpose'. Under the terms of their Agreement of 1712, he was to return to Saltoun and build a barley mill there in the Dutch style.

Using materials largely shipped over from Holland, Meikle in due course built the Saltoun barley mill, and later fanners too. Saltoun pearl barley soon became sought after. Business connected with the mill was conducted from an office in Edinburgh, and Margaret Carnegie herself took orders from an office in the mill. It was said that she kept the door of her room securely fastened in order to keep out prying eyes.

Certainly, James Meikle signed an undertaking not to reveal 'how the milne was framed and built', and he and the mill employees promised not to 'teach nor discover nor reveal to any one whatsomever, directly or indirectly the manner how the barley or pease or wheat or anyother thing that passes through the mill are shieled, separated, dight, fined, & made for sale'.[18] According to family legend, the secrets of the mill's construction and operation only became known when they were given away by a drunken employee some forty years later.

Henry Fletcher was the tenant of the mill, but it was his wife who was responsible for its success. In 1714, Henry wrote to his son, then a student at Leyden, that mother 'says you need not trouble yourself to inquire anything about the making of Barley, for she has taken pains on it since you went away and is perfectly master of it and the mill goes extraordinarily well'.[19] Not content with running the barley mill, Margaret went to the Netherlands to learn how to weave 'Holland cloth'. Subsequently, she set up a cloth-making business at Saltoun. The village was said to have been a hive of activity as a result of her enterprises. Andrew Fletcher went so far as to mourn that 'my brother has got the woman that should have been my wife'.[20]

The Saltoun mill husked barley, making it edible as meal. It could also be used as an ingredient in made-up dishes, notably in broths. The family recipe books include instructions for 'French Barley Cream' made with pearl barley as produced by the Saltoun mill. This is a rich, creamy, somewhat old-fashioned dish, thickened with blanched almonds and flavoured with spices and rosewater.

Advertisement for the Saltoun Barley Mill, eighteenth century.
Pearl barley from the Saltoun Mill was highly regarded.
National Library of Scotland, MS.17248, f.125.
By permission of J.T.T. Fletcher, of Saltoun.

Detail from a 'Plan of the Estate of Saltoun', showing the Saltoun Barley Mill, eighteenth century. National Library of Scotland, MS.17874 (22). By permission of J.T.T. Fletcher, of Saltoun.

[18] National Library of Scotland, Fletcher of Saltoun papers, MS.17248, ff.4-5.

[19] National Library of Scotland, Fletcher of Saltoun papers, MS.16503, f.77.

[20] *Recollections.*

FRENCH BARLEY CREAM

Take a porrenger full of pearll barly boill it in 8 or 9 several watters very tender then put in it a Choppen of sweet cream with some large mace and whole Cinnamon boill it ane quarter of ane hour then have two pound of Almonds bleanchd and beat fine with rose watter and as much suggar and work that in cold cream then put barley and all together on the fire and stirr it till it be ready to boill then take it off the fire still stearing it till it be half cold then put to it 3 spoonfulls of seck or whyt wine then eat it cold as all other milks must be.

Also among the Saltoun papers are a number of diagrams in the form of table plans. By the late seventeenth century increased concern with form and ritual had led cookery writers to stipulate exactly when and where each dish should be placed on the table.[21] Recipes for some of the dishes in the Saltoun diagrams appear in Margaret Carnegie's cookery books, suggesting that these particular meals may actually have been served to the Fletcher family.

As indicated by the plans, numerous and varied dishes were placed on the table at once. Diners generally helped themselves, but later servants might assist. Carving was usually done by the host. For the first course at the dinner shown here there was sago soup, sirloin of beef, saddle of mutton, or roast hindquarter of veal, together with a ragout of kernels, morello cherries, and truffles. The fourth dish was boiled or baked plum pudding, or something entirely different – lamb fricassee. When the soup had been consumed it was removed from the table and replaced by a hot flan with chickens and spinach. Dishes such as these were known as 'removes'.

The second course dishes are remarkably similar to those of the first, with roast geese or ducklings, tarts or lobsters, two roast pigs or chickens, and vegetable dishes of green peas and artichokes.

There was only one course for the lighter meal of supper. The meat part of this meal comprised dishes of boiled chickens and lemon sauce, lobsters, fried sole, or whiting, wild or tame roast fowl, and ragouts of Scots collops and sweetbreads. Also on the table were vegetable dishes of mushroom and artichoke fricassee, green peas, and artichokes. There was also an almond custard.

In Katharine Bruce and Margaret Carnegie the Fletcher of Saltoun family was blessed with two strong and respected women. In her cookery, the elder of the two was preoccupied with the preservation of fruit from the garden. Katherine's recipe book, begun in 1688, is much the same in its nature as that from Dunrobin a few years earlier. A later notebook shows her experimenting with new sauces and vegetable dishes, again trends in evidence at Dunrobin. This more adventurous approach was to be continued and developed by Margaret Carnegie when the family recipe books fell to her charge. It was she who brought the new drink, tea, soon to become so popular, to Saltoun. Like the Earls of Sutherland, the Fletchers were familiar with the Edinburgh and London scenes and were well aware of current trends. Outside this rarefied circle, things were very different.

Table-setting for a two course dinner, early eighteenth century. National Library of Scotland, MS.17853, ff.1v-2. *By permission of J.T.T. Fletcher, of Saltoun.*

[21] C. Anne Wilson, 'Ideal Meals and their Menus', in *The Appetite and the Eye,* ed. by C. Anne Wilson (Edinburgh, 1991), pp. 98-122. For table settings a century later, see below page 87.

Mrs. Johnston's
RECEIPTS
FOR
ll Sorts of Paſtry, Creams,
Puddings, Cuſtards, Preſerves,
Marmalets, Conſerves, Geillies,
Syrops, Wines, wet and dry Con-
fections, Biskets, Sauces, Pickles,
and Cookery,
After the neweſt and moſt approved
Method.

Edinburgh, Printed in the Year

4 SHEEP'S HEAD BROTH AND OYSTERS

OCHTERTYRE 1737-1739

MONDAY, 3 JANUARY 1737, 'KILLD A SHEEP, [BOUGHT] 2 DOZEN OF EGGS 4d, FOR MILK 1d'. So begins the 'House Booke of Accomps' of Ochtertyre and Fowlis, the Perthshire homes of Sir William Murray, 3rd Baronet of Ochtertyre.[1] Across the page, the 'Discharge' column records the dishes served for dinner that day: two soups, 'Sheep head broth' and 'fowls in the broth', were accompanied by boiled beef pieces, roast mutton joints and roast fowl. Later, supper consisted of goose giblets, roast mutton joints, minced pies and herrings, and 'eggs in the shell'.

Ochtertyre, in the parish of Monzievaird, belonged to the Murray family from the fifteenth century. Patrick Moray, the 1st Laird of Ochtertyre, died in 1476. The 3rd Laird, another Patrick, fell at Flodden in 1513. His son, David, also died fighting the English, this time at Pinkie in 1547. A family of good standing in the

Jeremiah Davison, 'Sir William Murray, 3rd Baronet of Ochtertyre'. By permission of Sotheby's.

[1] National Library of Scotland, Murray of Ochtertyre papers, MS.21106. For a modern version of the text of the House Book see James Colville, ed., 'The Ochtertyre House Booke of Accomps, 1737-9', *Scottish History Society*, 55 (Edinburgh, 1907).

prosperous county of Perthshire, William Murray was created a baronet by Charles II in 1673. By a Deed of Entail of 1726, the then Baronet ensured that no heir was to take a higher title on pain of forfeiture of his inheritance. The Murrays were destined to rise no further.

Succeeding generations of Murrays produced large numbers of children – the 3rd Baronet alone had nineteen – and the house at Ochtertyre must often have been too small for all the family and servants at once. Extra living space was much needed, and in 1667 the 1st Baronet purchased the estate of Fowlis Easter by Crieff. From this time, until Fowlis fell into disrepair and a new house was built at Ochtertyre in the early 1800s, the family moved regularly between their two homes.

Dating from 1737 to 1739, the 'Ochtertyre House Booke of Accomps' follows the family as they progress from one property to the other, recording incoming provisions and daily eating habits. Although the ancestral home of the Murrays was Ochtertyre, much of the two years covered by the House Book relates to Fowlis. When the accounts open in January 1737 the family was at Fowlis and moved to Ochterytre in September of that year. In January 1738 they were back at Fowlis, and from October 1738 until the sudden ending of the Book in January 1739 they stayed at Ochtertyre. Apart from being somewhat too small, the house at Ochtertyre was possibly in poor condition, given that it was pulled down soon after Robert Burns's visit in 1787. The visits to the old house at Ochtertyre in the autumn of each year took place principally for sport.

Sir William Murray, the Laird of Ochtertyre at the time of the House Book, was born at Fowlis Easter in 1682. According to the family history, he 'received a Liberal Education, and was bred at the University of Oxford and afterwards travelled in France and Italy. He was universally acclaimed as a Polite Scholar and Accomplished Gentleman'.[2] There were high hopes for his future.

Participation on the Jacobite side in the 1715 Rising led to Sir William's capture at the Battle of Sherriffmuir and subsequent imprisonment at Edinburgh and Carlisle. Although he was freed following the intervention of his father and maternal uncle, John Haldane of Gleneagles, many of Sir William's expectations were dashed. He was to have stood for election as Member of Parliament for Perthshire, but, the family history continues, 'having been concerned in the Rebellion in 1715 (at which time he was a very young man) it was determined on the night preceding the Election, to withdraw his Canvas'. In spite of this and other setbacks, Sir William succeeded his father in 1735 as the 3rd Baronet of Ochtertyre.

In 1706, Sir William married Katherine Fraser, daughter of Hugh, 9th Lord Lovat. Between 1707 and 1732 they had nineteen children, of whom twelve died in infancy. Although respectable and highly thought of, Sir William inherited little money from his father, and in 1729 his debts amounted to £42,000. This high level of indebtedness may well be reflected in the table kept at Ochtertyre and Fowlis. Nonetheless, debt did not keep Sir William at home, as the House Book frequently makes reference to letters despatched to him. Conversely, Lady Ochtertyre spent the greater part of her time at home with her young family. Sir William died in 1739, and Lady Ochtertyre lived on at Fowlis until her death in 1771.

[2] National Library of Scotland, Murray of Ochtertyre papers, MS.21116, f.38.

Drawing by Timothy Ross of Fowlis Easter Castle, c.1880.
Although Ochtertyre was the Murray's ancestral home, the family spent much of their time at Fowlis. *National Library of Scotland, MS.712, no.114.*

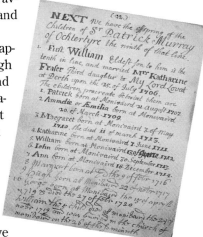

Genealogical notes relating to Sir William Murray, taken from the 'Family book of the Murrays of Ochtertyre', eighteenth century. National Library of Scotland, MS.21115, f.13.

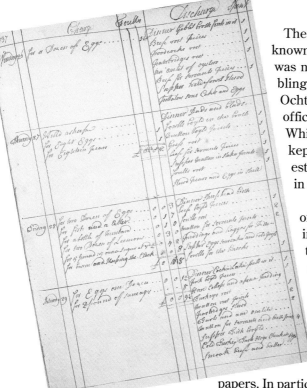

'The Ochtertyre House Booke of Accomps', 1737-1739.
The Ochtertyre House Book follows the Murray family as they progress between Fowlis and Ochtertyre, recording both incoming provisions and daily eating habits.
National Library of Scotland, MS.21106.

The identity of the writer of the 'Ochtertyre House Booke' is unknown, but the few personal details that do appear indicate that it was not a member of the family. References to expenses for stabling horses at Perth and for 'the lads and myself coming to Ochtertyre' suggest the Book was written by a male servant whose office corresponded to that of the house steward at Dunrobin. While the records of incoming provisions and daily menus were kept in separate volumes at Dunrobin, at the Murray's smaller establishment they were combined in the one book, as happened in the Earl of Angus's household.

The 'Ochtertyre House Booke' has its limitations as a source of dietary information: there are no accompanying recipes, no indication of numbers catered for, and little information as to the quantity of food prepared. The numbers of joints of meat and small animals and birds such as chickens, hares, pigeons, and partridges taken to the table are recorded, but many of the entries give no more information than 'fish with mustard sauce' or 'an omlit and a salad'.

Although the House Book does not provide a complete record of the eating habits of Sir William Murray and his family, additional information appears among the family papers. In particular, the 'Inventory of Household furniture belonging to Sir Patrick Murray of Ochtertyre 9 July 1763' compiled on the death of the 4th Baronet, is a useful source.[3]

This inventory paints a vivid picture of the dining room at Ochtertyre. There were twelve 'elme' chairs with black-leather seats, a large mahogany table and a number of smaller side tables. A mahogany cooler for wine took pride of place, and heating came from a fire with a polished grate. On the walls were family portraits and a map of Germany. Clearly, the family ate in some comfort and style.

Despite the presence of the large dining table and four smaller tables, the dining room was not used exclusively for eating, as the inventory lists '1 Bagaman [backgammon] Table with men and Dices'. The drawing room also had multiple functions as it contained an 'India Tea Table', presumably for the use of Lady Ochtertyre and her female relatives and guests.

The kitchen section of the inventory is longer than that for any other room in the house. The family pewter is listed first. This consisted of 'one Pewdder Supp [soup] dish', '23 Dishes of Different sizes', and '2 Pewdder fish plats'. Copperware included stew pans, a fish kettle, a sauce pan, ladles, and scummers. In addition, there were iron frying pans and iron pots both large and small. Iron spits and racks were used for roasting joints of meat, and an iron 'jack with two chains' for suspending pots and pans over the open fire. There were two ovens: a 'batchlers oven' in the kitchen and another in the Bake House. The picture is completed by an assortment of small items including '3 hair searches [sieves]', knives, 'a flesh fork', a grater, collop tongs,[4] 'a flaming spoon', rolling pin and a number of measuring jugs.

[3] National Library of Scotland, Murray of Ochtertyre papers, MS.21110, ff.30-5.

[4] Collop tongs were instruments used for holding chops over the fire.

The 'service area' of the house included a number of smaller rooms each with its own function. There was a 'Milk House', a 'Brew House', a 'Bottle Court', a 'Bake House', and several cellars. An establishment of this size must have boasted a considerable number of servants. The inventory confirms this, listing the contents of the Housekeeper's Room and the Butler's Pantry. Mention is also made of the 'Cook's dress' and the servants' sleeping quarters.

In many respects, the butler's role evolved out of that of the house steward and the chamberlain. He kept records of incoming provisions, food issued from the stores, and completed dishes sent up to the dining room. He was also in charge of the male servants. The Butler's Pantry was home to the family silver including '10 harts horn hafted knives' and twelve forks and the family's four oyster knives. His responsibility now extended to supervision of the cellar and glass-ware. This important servant was probably the author of the House Book.

Unfortunately, no manuscript recipe book of the family has survived, if indeed there ever was one. However, recipes for many of the dishes served at Ochtertyre appear in two contemporary cookery books: *Mrs McLintock's Receipts for Cookery and Pastry-Work* (published in Glasgow in 1736), and *Mrs Johnston's Receipts for all sorts of Pastry, Creams, Puddings, Custards, Preserves, Marmalets, Conserves, Geillies, Syrops, Wines, wet and dry Confections, Biskets, Sauces, Pickles and Cookery, After the newest and most approved Methods* which appeared in Edinburgh in about 1740.

Both Mrs McLintock and Mrs Johnston lean towards medieval cookery in their heavy use of almonds, cream, eggs, and spices. There are some new recipes for fricassees and ragouts and notably 'Beef Alamode the French Way'. Generally, both avoid French terminology, referring to 'leg of lamb' not the French 'gigot', giving weight to the view that French influence on Scottish cookery was not of great importance prior to the late eighteenth century. These, the earliest recipe books published in Scotland, are almost contemporary, and are identical in many

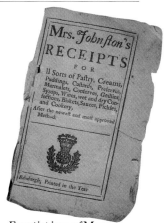

Frontispiece of Mrs Johnston's Receipts for all sorts of Pastry, Creams, Puddings, Custards, Preserves . . . After the Newest and Most Approved Methods (Edinburgh, 1740). National Library of Scotland.

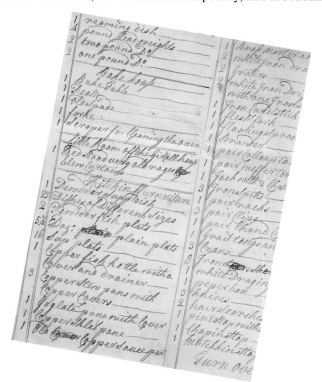

'Kitchen Furniture' at Ochtertyre. From the 'Inventory of household furniture belonging to Sir Patrick Murray of Ochtertyre 9 July 1763'. National Library of Scotland, MS.21110, f.33v.

The 'Butler's Pantry' at Ochtertyre. From the 'Inventory of the Household furniture belonging to Sir Patrick Murray of Ochtertyre 9 July 1763'. The Butler's Pantry was home to the family's silverware, cutlery and glassware.
National Library of Scotland, MS.21110, f.34v.

respects. Mrs McLintock and Mrs Johnston may well be one and the same person.

Meat in one form or another continues to dominate the diet. Large quantities were involved, and much of the flesh served at Ochtertyre and Fowlis was taken from the 'spent' or larder. By this time, important houses had separate store-rooms for food, usually adjacent to the kitchen. At Ochtertyre, no one room was designated as a larder as such. Rather, food in store was divided between several service rooms, namely the 'ale bottle seller [cellar]', the 'Guile House' and the 'Little Room off the Girnal [the meal store]'. Smaller houses had to make do with ventilated cupboards. In some Highland houses wickerwork panels were inserted into the sides of the cupboards to provide the necessary ventilation.

Mutton in particular dominates the meals described in the House Book. The accounts open with the words 'Killd a sheep'. The animal was probably then hung for some time. Lamb or mutton from the family estates was plentiful, and for dinner that same day 'sheep head broth' and 'mutton rost joints' were on the menu. The roast joints made a repeat appearance at supper, and again the following day. 'Mutton boyld joints' were served for dinner on the Tuesday and for supper on the Wednesday. On the Thursday another sheep was killed.

Sheep's head broth was a favourite at Ochtertyre. A well-known Scottish dish, it consists of barley broth with an entire singed sheep's head stewed in it. Traditionally, it was served with the head taking pride of place in the middle of the bowl. Later, and especially when the dish was exported south of the Border, the head was chopped into pieces to make it acceptable to more sensitive souls. A substantial, nourishing dish, sheep's head broth was popular in Scotland then and for years to come.

Sheep had been kept in Scotland for centuries, but their primary purpose was to provide wool and milk. As far as the ordinary Scot was concerned, sheep were eaten when they died, be it of natural causes or disease. Only the very wealthy could afford regularly to slaughter their animals for food and eat meat on a daily basis. Despite this, mutton, the favourite meat dish at Ochtertyre, was the most commonly eaten flesh in Scotland.

Beef, in the form of either roasted or boiled joints, followed by 'cold beefe sliced', made daily appearances on the dining table alongside mutton. At Ochtertyre and Fowlis, although the occasional side of beef was bought, the cattle eaten generally belonged to the family. Like the sheep, cattle, too, were not primarily kept for eating: their function was to serve as draught animals and to provide milk. From time to time, the weights of joints of meat are noted. The wide variations in size between one animal and another indicate the poor condition of the herd. These animals were far removed in breeding and condition from the beef and dairy herds of today.

The 'Slaughter House', mentioned in the household inventory of some thirty

years later, confirms that animals were killed on the premises. In 1737, 'a slaughter axe' and 'a large cleaver' were bought. Comments such as, at harvest time, 'Cutt sixe Leges of Cooper beef Into 30 pieces for servants and the shearers Leading in the Corns' bring the dry accounts to life.

When an animal had recently been killed or butcher-meat bought in, the meat served was probably fresh. Otherwise, it was preserved and stored against future use. Purchases of salt and vinegar show that here too meat was salted and pickled. These time-consuming processes usually took place away from the kitchen. The 1763 inventory lists '2 stands for pickling pork' in the 'ale bottle cellar' and '2 stands with Covers for salting beeff' in the 'Barle [barley] Ale seller'.

Another favourite method of preserving meat was collaring, and instructions for collaring are given in most eighteenth-century recipe books. The lengthy procedure of collaring involved boning the animal, seasoning the flesh with pepper, nutmeg, mace, salt, and lemon-peel, and then rolling the meat, tying it tightly ('tye it up strait with broad knittings'), and boiling until tender (together with the head and feet) in a pan of salted water. The meat was then left to drain and cool before being immersed in vinegar and yet more seasonings. At this point, sweet herbs, such as sage, thyme, and bay leaves could be added if desired. Once treated in this manner, meat would stay fresh for up to six months.

At Ochtertyre both beef and pork were served collared. Pigs were killed regularly, sometimes as many as four at once: '2 to roast and 2 for collaring' is the usual comment. Roast or boiled pig, hams, collared pig, and sausages were all eaten. Pork in one form or another was consumed frequently alongside the mutton and beef. Once again, there seems to have been no prejudice against pork.

Drying was a much simpler method of preservation. Widely used in Scotland, it involves drawing out the liquid which would otherwise cause decomposition. A fifteenth-century visitor to Scotland, Vidame de Chartres, wrote that the Scots ate raw venison which had been pressed between two pieces of wood until it became hard and dry. Others air-dried flesh or fish by simply hanging it up to dry. According to Martin Martin, who visited St Kilda in 1698, the islanders dried solan geese and gannets 'in their storehouses, without any salt or spices to preserve them'.[5] So treated, the birds would keep for up to a year, being boiled or roasted before eating.

The process of drying could be speeded up by placing flesh before the fire. At the same time as drying out the meat, smoke gives it a distinctive flavour. Now and then, smoked beef appears on the supper menu at Ochtertyre, but never at dinner-time. 'Smokt beef with eggs' was served in October 1737, a few weeks later 'smokt beef and pickles', and in the spring of 1738 'smoakt beef and butter' appears. Given that on all these days the menus were unusually lengthy and elaborate, the family was probably entertaining and special menus were devised. Smoked meat was a delicacy served on special occasions.

Once an animal was killed, the family ate the flesh until it had all been consumed. In his *Reminiscences of Scottish Life and Character*, Dean Ramsay tells the story of a dinner party given by a Scottish judge at which all the dishes were based on veal: veal broth, roast fillet of veal, veal cutlets, a calf's head, and calf's

'The Ochtertyre House Booke of Accomps', 1737-1739.
National Library of Scotland, MS.21106.

[5] Martin, p. 441.

foot jelly. On seeing the looks on the faces of his guests, he announced, 'Ou aye, it's a cauf. When we kill a beast, we just eat up ae side and doun the tither'.[6] Even in a Laird's house fresh meat was at too much of a premium for anything to go to waste. 'Hog's [a fat sheep] cheek', 'Tongue and lure [udder] rost', 'tripe fricassee', and 'puddings eggs and sweetbreads' all put in an appearance in the accounts. Virtually every part of the animal was eaten.

As might be expected, the servants received more than their fair share of the less choice dishes: 'hoges head and feet for the servants', 'the cows hart [heart] and breeds [sweetbreads] for the servants', and 'the cows draught [entrail] for the servants', contrast with the roasts and steaks for the family. Haggis, served regularly at Dunrobin, appears here only once as 'Puddings and hagas for serv[an]ts'. Separate servants' menus are not a feature of every meal here, and when they do appear, joints of boiled beef and mutton are the norm. Probably, they were expected to eat the left-overs from the family's meal.

Occasionally, the servants at Ochtertyre were given cheese for supper, but, as at Dunrobin, cheese was not served to the family, suggesting that it was not highly regarded. As late as 1826 the Scottish cookery writer Margaret (Meg) Dods referred to cheese-making as 'this tardy branch of our rural economy'.[7] Her deprecating remarks about Scottish cheese were probably made in comparison with the situation in England where cheese-making was widespread, both commercially and in the home. There, numerous distinctive regional cheeses were produced and marketed. While locally produced cheese was not held in great esteem north of the Border, some English cheeses were exported to Scotland: the Fletcher of Saltoun accounts note a Cheshire cheese bought in 1722.[8]

The famous Stilton cheese was first sold at the Bell Inn, a coaching inn on the Great North Road at Stilton in Leicestershire, and so must have been sampled by travellers between Scotland and England. Its widespread popularity led to numerous imitations. Recipes for Stilton cheese made their way into Scottish cookery books. Jean Robinson's 'Pastry Book', begun in Elgin in 1734,[9] and the 'Kinfauns Castle Receipt Book'[10] of the late eighteenth century both feature Stilton recipes.

The first 'sweet milk' or full-cream hard cheese of Scotland probably came from the Ayrshire village of Dunlop. Lying in the mild, wet, south-west corner of Scotland, this area has suitable climatic conditions for cheese-making, and the Ayrshire cattle are known for their high yields and quality of milk. Tradition has it that Barbara Gilmour first made Dunlop cheese. This farmer's wife from Ireland settled in the village in 1688. Whatever its origins, Dunlop was marketed in several Scottish towns. As a cheese which would both keep and travel, in the course of the eighteenth century, it rapidly displaced skim-milk and sheep's milk cheese.

Chickens, capons, ducks, geese, turkeys, pigeons, and partridges: poultry of one sort or another was on the table every day in the Murray household. Rarely purchased, some of these birds came as gifts from friends: Lord Gray sent six

[6] Edward Ramsay, *Reminiscences of Scottish Life and Character* (Edinburgh, 1857).

[7] Margaret Dods, *The Cook and Housewife's Manual* (Edinburgh, 1826), p. 343.

[8] National Library of Scotland, Fletcher of Saltoun papers, MS.17082, f.30.

[9] National Library of Scotland, MS.24775, f.18.

[10] National Library of Scotland, MS.24778, p.11.

partridges in August 1737. The majority must have been given as rent in kind from tenants or have come from the hen-house at Fowlis. Turkeys were killed at any time of year, but ducks and geese were seasonal: roast ducklings were served in summer, and muscovys in September. Usually, they were roasted or boiled; later the remains were served up cold from the larder.

'Foulls' or capons were by far the most common poultry dishes. 'Foulls in the soup', 'foulls rost', 'foulls spent' (cold from the larder), and 'foulls broyld' are all common. Sometimes, 'fouls for the hawks' appears alongside the list of dishes for the family. Perhaps these birds were surplus to requirements.

In the early autumn of 1738, the Ochtertyre doocot provided numerous meals. During September and October over a hundred and eighty pigeons were received with the comment 'from the doocot'. Pigeon pie, requiring no fewer than twelve pigeons for each pie, was a favourite served weekly. Highly seasoned with nutmeg and cloves as well as salt and pepper, these pies were sealed with butter to aid preservation. Between pies, pigeons appeared on the table variously roasted, boiled, or potted.

The House Book is careful to distinguish between birds reared in the hen-run and wild fowl. So, 'wilde ducks' are carefully noted, as is the occasional solan goose. Woodcocks, moorfowl, blackbirds, teal, plovers, snipe, and partridges all feature. Regular entries such as 'To powder and shot to Joseph' show how commonplace and important in the diet hunting and shooting were. When they reached the kitchen, these wild birds were usually roasted or boiled. As delicacies, partridges were given more sophisticated treatment, and might be stewed with celery in an oyster sauce.

(68)

140. To make a Frigacy of Rabbets, or Chickens.

When ye have cut them in Pieces, blanch them a little in cold Water, then fry them a little, and drain them from the Greafe; and take as much Veal Broth, as will cover them in the Pan, boil your Spices in the Broth the Sauce is made of, when the Sauce is boiled to what you would have it, beat the Yolks of 4 or 5 Eggs, a Nutmeg grated, 4 or 5 Spoonfuls of White-wine, fharpen it to your Tafte with a little Vinegar; cut Parfly, a few Oyfters, give them all a boil with your Frigacy; then put in the Yolks of the Eggs, and tofs them up, and put the Capers and Cucumbers on the Top.

141. To make a Ragou of Veal or Lamb.

Take the Back-ribs of Veal or Lamb, and cut them two Ribs together, fpread them on a Table, and beat them with the rolling Pin, flower them, and fry them, take out the Shoulder-Bone, and roll up your Flefh in a Colleur with Spices, and fry it very well; then drain them from the Greafe, and take the

Extract from Mrs Johnston's Receipts *(Edinburgh, 1740)*. Mrs Johnston's recipe for chicken or rabbit fricassee involved searing the meat before cooking, a method new to Scotland. *National Library of Scotland.*

Such made-up dishes (combinations of ingredients cooked together) were now well established in Scotland, and 'chicken fricasie', as served at Dunrobin in 1703, was a regular on the table at Ochtertyre. Mrs Johnston's recipe for the dish is much the same as that given by Lady Castlehill in 1711, save that the pieces of chicken were first fried in butter rather than boiled. Searing meat before cooking was a method new to Scotland, but one which was growing rapidly in popularity. Oysters, capers, and cucumbers completed the dish.[11] Mrs Johnston's recipe was for fricassee of chicken or rabbit. At Ochtertyre both chicken and rabbit fricassee were served, and the occasional 'fricasie of tripe' appeared at supper-time.

The thickening agent used in the new sauces was usually egg yolk. As well as being important ingredients in made-up dishes, eggs were on the menu virtually every day at both Ochtertyre and Fowlis. At this time, most wealthy households had their own hen-runs and received large numbers of eggs as rent in kind. Egg dishes provided a ready and cheap means of nourishment.

While this was the case for the wealthy, it was not so for the common people. So many eggs produced in Scotland were given as rent-money that they did not routinely form a part of the diet before the nineteenth century. Only when payments of rent in kind ceased to be the norm did eggs come within daily reach of the populace.[12]

The regular incoming and home-produced eggs together were still insufficient to meet the demands of the Murray family, and large quantities of eggs at three pence for two dozen were bought. So, the numerous egg dishes were not served simply to use up stocks: there must have been a deliberate decision to buy and serve them. Perhaps someone in the Murray family was particularly fond of eggs.

'Eggs in the shell' (boiled eggs) was by far the most frequently served egg dish, but eggs were also served as accompaniments to a wide range of dishes. Combinations with meat such as 'eggs and collared pigs', 'cold goose and eggs', and 'eggs and cold beefe' all appear. Eggs were served with vegetables such as potatoes, artichokes and spinach. They also appear with fish, especially herrings. Sometimes, they were combined with shell-fish to produce the intriguing 'eggs and grave [gravy] and a parton [crab] pie'. The less fortunate servants were simply served a plate of eggs.

The cooking method for these egg dishes was not usually specified, possibly because the writer saw no need to state what to him was the obvious. However, on 24 March 1738, 'Trout and eggs buttered' was on the menu. Frying in fat was one of the standard methods of cooking eggs at this time. We are not to know if the method was noted here simply because it was out of the ordinary for this particular household. Apart from frying, the most usual method of cooking eggs out of their shells was by poaching in hot water or broth.

Eggs were served all year round, and it is possible that some were preserved. Preservation of eggs was achieved by first coating them in a substance such as butter or oil to seal them, and then packing them in bran or sawdust.[13] Treated in this way, eggs would keep for several months.

[11] *Mrs Johnston's Receipts for all sorts of Pastry, Creams, Puddings, Custards, Preserves. . . After the Newest and Most Approved Methods* (Edinburgh, 1740), p. 47.

[12] Hope, *A Caledonian Feast*, p. 156.

[13] Brears, p. 58.

The egg dishes at Ochtertyre and Fowlis were always served at supper-time, never at dinner. The importance of light, easily digestible, egg dishes in the supper menus of the Murray family may be of some significance. Eggs appear far less frequently in the Dunrobin Diet Book, and their popularity in Perthshire some thirty years later serves to confirm the trend towards a lighter meal in the afternoon or early evening, a practice which became increasingly established as the century wore on.

In the autumn and winter months when the family was in residence at Ochtertyre, considerable numbers of hares were either shot or trapped for the pot. The standard dish was roast hare at dinner, but 'hares in soupe', stewed hares, hare pies, and 'hare collops' were also served. Collops must have been popular, as venison, beef, mutton, kidney, and veal as well as hare collops are all mentioned. Collop tongs, for holding chops over the fire, were bought for sixpence in 1738. Perhaps these are the same tongs listed in the household inventory some fifteen years later. Rabbits, so popular at Dunrobin, were rarely served, and when they do appear they are bought in, suggesting that there was no rabbit warren on the Ochtertyre estate.

Fish, too, was bought frequently and served almost daily. Now and then there is mention of the gift of a salmon. While both dried and fresh fish are mentioned, a far greater variety of fresh fish was consumed at Ochtertyre than at Dunrobin. Generally, fish was served with greater imagination here. So, there is 'salmon with green sauce', 'salmon with fryed soals [sole]', 'herring and fryed apple', 'fish with mustard sauce', 'fish stewed', 'fryed flounder', 'perches with kidney beans' and 'hard fish with eggs'.

Shell-fish were popular too. While there is the occasional lobster and crab, oysters continued to be both plentiful and cheap. On 10 September 1737, two hundred oysters were bought for just one shilling and sixpence. Eggs and scalloped oysters were on the supper table that evening. The following day there were partridges with an oyster sauce. No further mention is made of oysters on subsequent days, and it may be that the entire two hundred were eaten over the two days.

Scottish oysters enjoyed a considerable reputation. In the 1780s, Faujas de St Foord, the French Commissioner of Wines, commented on the 'plumpness and exquisite flavour' of the oysters he was served at Prestonpans, adding that they were so fine that they were exported in barrels throughout England and Wales.[14]

Oyster gauges.
Gauges were used to determine the size of individual oysters, and from that, their cost.
Huntly House Museum, Edinburgh.

[14] McNeill, p. 22.

Vegetables appear at Ochtertyre and Fowlis both as separate dishes and as accompaniments (as at Dunrobin in the early 1700s). However, the menus in this Perthshire household some thirty years later place a far greater emphasis on them. As no purchases or gifts of vegetables are recorded, what was eaten was probably the produce of the kitchen gardens.

Traditional broths such as hodge podge, cock-a-leekie, and sheep's head broth were the most commonly eaten soups, but vegetable soups such as celery and 'green soup' were also served at Ochtertyre. In Mrs Johnston's cookery book the latter included spinach. First, beef and onions were boiled with a marrow bone and sweet herbs and spices until the meat fell to pieces. The liquid broth was then strained through a colander. Next, the juice from beaten fresh spinach was added, and the broth cooked over a slow fire. It was then poured into a soup dish over 'some toasted bread' and served.

Vegetables as varied as artichokes, peas, French beans, kidney beans, asparagus, savoy cabbages, spinach, celery, and potatoes are all mentioned as accompaniments to meat, poultry, game, fish, and eggs in what seems like an infinite number of combinations. Celery was served with partridges, beans with fish and bacon, and savoys with cold beef and puddings. Spinach was teamed with eggs, as indeed were peas. The latter also appear with crab and haggis. These three dishes were served on four consecutive days in June 1737 when there must have been a glut of peas. Now and then, there is mention of a 'sallad'. 'Pease and a sallad and a lobster' sounds particularly enticing. Sometimes, vegetables were added to the sauce of a made-up dish, although the 'green sauce' to accompany salmon could have been made either of spinach or apples. Various vegetable 'puddings' appear as separate dishes, pease pudding and carrot pudding being the most common.

'Potato pudding' is one of a series of puddings served. Many of these were based on vegetables, the same recipe being used for such diverse ingredients as bread, rice, almonds, carrots, and oranges. First, the main ingredient was cooked until tender, then mashed and mixed with a dozen egg yolks, and a quantity of sweet cream and butter; finally, currants, cinnamon, and sugar to taste were added.

Potatoes appear in the Ochtertyre menus regularly from August until March. At Dunrobin, they were served occasionally and then only at supper either as a separate dish or perhaps with fritters. Here, potatoes usually appear as an accompaniment: in January with cold ham, in February with tripe, in August with artichokes, and in September with stewed peas and greens. The cooking method is not specified, but they were probably boiled and then peeled and cooked on the fire with butter, as recommended by John Reid.

Field cultivation of potatoes had begun in Scotland by the 1720s. In 1726, the noted agricultural improver John Cockburn of Ormiston planted them in a tenant's field. However, their cultivation outside the gardens of the wealthy did not become generally accepted until at least the 1760s. By then, as Henry Somerville writes, potatoes were considered 'a very bulky and valuable food for the whole of the lower ranks, and a substitute for bread at the tables of all the superior ranks'.

At Ochtertyre, the impression given is that this was far from the case in the 1730s. While served too often to be considered a delicacy, potatoes remained something of a novelty. In March, some of the last potatoes of the season were served in a pie. The recipe for this pie has not survived, and neither of the two cookery books published in Scotland at about this time includes potato recipes. However, as is so often the case, a manuscript recipe book may more accurately reflect current trends. Jean Robinson's 'Pastry Book' begun in 1734 includes two potato recipes: 'A Florentine [a plate pie] of Apples with Potatoes or Chastines [chestnuts]', and a recipe for a potato pudding.[15]

The florentine recipe applies medieval principles to the new vegetable: raisins or currants, blanched almonds, seasonings of sugar and cinnamon, together with lemon and orange-peel were added to the layers of sliced apples and boiled sliced potatoes. White wine was poured over the assembled dish, and a puff-pastry lid added before baking. Rather than being tasty and filling accompaniments, potatoes are treated here almost as a sweetmeat.

25
TO MAKE A FFLORENTINE OF APPLES WITH POTATOS OR CHASTINES

Take your Apples pair and Cut them in thin Slices, keeping the hearts & take your Potatos being boiled Skin & Cut them as you did your Apples & take half a pound either of Raisens or Curranes and haff a pound of blenched Almonds & half a pound of Sugar two drops of Cinnamon four Ounces of Citron & orange peel then rub the bottom of your Dish with Butter and lay a Lair of Sugar between them till you have put in all you design & your dish be full, then pour in a Mutchkine of Whitewine & Cover it with puft past and so bake it, the Chastines are done as the Potatoes but they are not both to be put in the one Dish.

Recipe for a 'Fflorentine of Apples with Potatos or Chastines' from Jean Robinson's 'Pastry Book', Elgin 1743.
Jean Robinson's 'Pastry Book' includes two recipes for potatoes: one for a potato pudding, and the other for an apple and potato florentine or pie.
National Library of Scotland, MS.24775, f.7.

[15] National Library of Scotland, MS.24775, f.7.

Fresh fruit puts in an infrequent appearance in made-up dishes at Ochtertyre. A pudding with fruit is mentioned, as is 'French beans and an apple tart'. Apples, too, were served. They could be fried with herring and perhaps featured in the green sauce accompanying salmon. Oranges and lemons were bought in when required and used in sauces or to make sweet dishes such as 'orange pudding'. As it was necessary to purchase apples and pears, Ochtertyre and Fowlis probably did not have their own fruit orchards. Without a seasonal glut to eat or preserve, the Murray household did not place great emphasis on the consumption of fresh fruit.

As in the Earl of Angus's household in 1608, although to a lesser degree, far more dried fruit than fresh was bought in. Currants and raisins appear in the accounts. Spices such as nutmeg, mace, and cloves were bought, also rice, almonds, and rosewater. At Ochtertyre, as in the published and manuscript recipe books of the time, the influence of medieval methods of cookery continued.

The impression given by the 'Ochtertyre House Booke' is of a well-to-do, but not extravagant, Scottish baronial household. The fare consisted of plain, traditional, Scottish cooking with abundant meat, poultry, game, fresh fish, and produce from the kitchen garden. This was enlivened by a few fashionable sauce-based dishes, mostly French in origin. Food seems to have been plentiful, if not lavish. Delicacies were served, but not on a daily basis, being treats kept for special occasions, usually when guests were present. This is a very human record of the daily routine of rural life in a laird's household: one in which 'a pair of shoos to the brewer' is given equal prominence with the chicken fricassee served at supper.

A

NEW AND EASY

METHOD

OF

COOKERY.

TREATING,

I. Of GRAVIES, SOUPS, | IV. OF PIES, PASTIES,
BROTHS, &c. | &c.
II. Of FISH, and their | V. OF PICKLING and
SAUCES. | PRESERVING.
III. To Pot and Make | VI. Of Made WINES, DI-
HAMS, &c. | STILLING and BREW-
| ING, &c.

TO WHICH ARE ADDED,

By Way of APPENDIX,

Fifty-Three NEW and USEFUL RECEIPTS,
and DIRECTIONS for CARVING.

By ELIZABETH CLELAND.

Chiefly intended for the Benefit of the Young LADIES
who attend Her SCHOOL.

The SECOND EDITION.

EDINBURGH:

Printed by C. WRIGHT and COMPANY: And sold at their
Printing-house in Craig's Closs, and by the Booksellers in Town.
M.DCC.LIX.

5 COOKERY SCHOOLS AND CHEESECAKES

EDINBURGH, 1752-1758

'SPRING SOUP',[1] 'ESCARLOT BEEF', 'EGG CHEESE-CAKES', 'MACAROONS' – THESE RECIPES, taken from Elizabeth Cleland's *A New and Easy Method of Cookery* of 1755, are far removed from the simple food produced at Ochtertyre some twenty years earlier. Annette Hope writes that, in the mid-eighteenth century, 'a new approach to cookery was now influencing the fashionable world at the centre of which Edinburgh – thanks to a sudden and dramatic flowering of original talent – was now placing itself'.[2]

At this time, Edinburgh, or the 'Athens of the North' as it later became known, nurtured many great minds. David Hume the philosopher, Robert Adam the ar-

Allan Ramsay, 'Margaret Erskine, Lady Alva'. By courtesy of the Lord Craigmyle.

[1] Mrs Cleland's Spring Soup was made from lettuce, cucumber, and young peas. Later, it might include rhubarb stalks (for which see page 76).

[2] Hope, *A Caledonian Feast*, p. 239.

chitect, William Robertson the historian, and many more made the town their home. Although it no longer had the same status as before James VI and I left for London in 1603, lawyers, medical men, and academics still thronged to Edinburgh. In the Season, their numbers were swelled by the ranks of Scotland's aristocrats and gentry who maintained town houses in the capital.

The household of the lawyer James Erskine of Alva was typical of Edinburgh's numerous legal families. Born in 1723, James Erskine was the son of a lawyer and the grandson of a Perthshire baronet. In 1749, he married his first wife Margaret Maguire, daughter and co-heir of Hugh Maguire of Drumdow, in Ayrshire. In 1754, James was made a Baron of the Exchequer, and in 1761 was raised to the Bench as Lord Barjarg. Later he became Lord Alva. Margaret died in 1766, but James remarried and lived on until 1796, when he died at the advanced age of seventy-three.

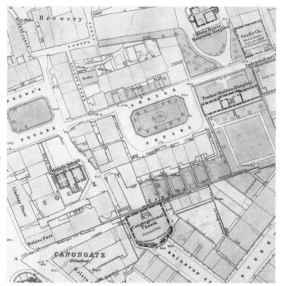

Argyle Square, Edinburgh. Detail from 'Edinburgh and its Environs', Ordnance Survey, 1:1056, published 1852-1855. Argyle Square was one of the first developments built to alleviate the congestion and over-crowding of Edinburgh's Old Town. It was demolished in the 1860s to make way for Chambers Street. *National Library of Scotland.*

The Erskine family seat was at Alva in Stirlingshire, but for much of the year the demands of the legal profession kept James and Margaret in their Edinburgh town house in Argyle Square. Lying to the south of the High Street, Argyle Square was completed in about 1742, and was one of the earliest of the developments built to alleviate the congestion and over-crowding of the Old Town.[3] Light, airy, spacious town houses such as these were a novelty for Edinburgh citizens. So unusual was this style of building that Sir John Clerk of Eldin commented in tones of some amazement that the Square was built 'after the fashion of London, every house being designed for only one family'.[4]

Although enthusiasm for the new housing was not universal, the Erskines were accompanied in their move to Argyle Square by others from the cream of Edinburgh society.[5] In 1752, one of the larger houses belonged to Mr Wauchope of Edmistone and yet another to Sir John Whitefoord. As was typical of Edinburgh, the residents of the Square came from a wide social mix, and in 1752 included merchants, brewers, a bookbinder, a wright, and a stabler.

The wealthy and professional people who flocked to Edinburgh wanted the best education for their children and were prepared to pay for it. Such was the demand that, in the course of the eighteenth century, large numbers of private schools were established, including some specifically for girls. Of the pupils at these schools, many would go on to run their own establishments, while the less fortunate were employed as senior servants. The subjects offered suggest that many of the schools were intended as finishing schools for girls who had received the rudiments of an education elsewhere.

One such young lady was Margaret Erskine's sister, Jacobina Maguire, who attended classes in music, singing, dancing, and French when she stayed with the family in Argyle Square between 1751 and 1755.[6] These were undoubtedly the

[3] Argyle Square appears on William Edgar's plan of Edinburgh of 1746.

[4] John Fleming, *Robert Adam and his Circle in Edinburgh and Rome* (London, 1962), p. 86.

[5] James Gilhooley, *A Directory of Edinburgh in 1752* (Edinburgh, 1988).

[6] National Library of Scotland, MS.5101, ff.1-22.

Advertisement in The Caledonian Mercury *of 16 June 1759 announcing the publication of the second edition of Elizabeth Cleland's* A New and Easy Method of Cookery. *National Library of Scotland.*

most commonly taught subjects, but the Edinburgh directories and newspapers show that lessons were available in numerous other subjects, including cookery.

At least eight Edinburgh schools taught cookery at some time in the eighteenth century.[7] The earliest such school was that of Mr Hautbois, teacher of cookery and pastry and 'Late cook to the Earl of Albemarle'. His school operated in the Canongate in the 1740s. Another cookery school was run between 1749 and 1752 by a Mrs Johnston. She later opened a boarding school for girls, and may well have been the author of Mrs Johnston's cookery book considered in Chapter 4. Mrs Wilkie operated a specialist pastry school in Marlin's Wynde from 1749 to 1758. Yet another cookery school was that run by Elizabeth Cleland.

In 1755, Mrs Cleland's book, *A New and Easy Method of Cookery*, was advertised in the *Caledonian Mercury* as being 'chiefly intended for the Benefit of the Young Ladies who attend Her School'. Unfortunately, no indication as to the school's location is given. The book proved popular, with second and third editions appearing in 1759 and 1770; even Sir Walter Scott had a copy in his library at Abbotsford. Containing a mix of traditional Scottish recipes and sophisticated new dishes from as far afield as France, Holland, Poland, Switzerland and England, Elizabeth Cleland's work reflects the changing face of cookery among wealthy Scots.[8]

Mrs Cleland's book is comprehensive. There are chapters on 'Gravies, soups and Broths', 'Fish and their Sauces', how 'To Pot and Make Hams', 'Of Pies, Pasties', 'Of Pickling and Preserves', and 'Of making Wines, Distilling and Brewing'. The appendix consists of no fewer than 'Fifty-Three New and Useful RECEIPTS, AND DIRECTIONS for CARVING'. While Mrs McLintock's and Mrs Johnston's cookery books, published only a few years earlier, had been presented haphazardly, Mrs Cleland's work is highly organised, being divided into sections and with an index at the back. In this respect, it more closely resembles present-day recipe books.

Elizabeth Cleland, A New and Easy Method of Cookery *(Edinburgh, 1759).*
Elizabeth Cleland ran one of at least eight cookery schools in eighteenth-century Edinburgh.
National Library of Scotland.

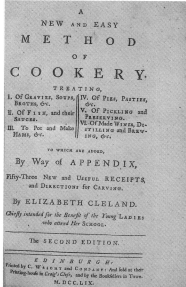

[7] Alexander Law, 'Teachers in Edinburgh in the Eighteenth Century', in *The Book of the Old Edinburgh Club*, 32 (1966), 108-57.

[8] Virginia Maclean, *A Short-title Catalogue of Household and Cookery Books Published in the English Tongue, 1701-1800* (London, 1981), p. 27.

Organisation of material in recipe books was not new. The first printed cookery book arranged according to logical principles was written by the Englishwoman Hannah Glasse.[9] Her *Art of Cookery Made Plain and Easy*, first published in London in 1747, was extremely well received. So successful was it that Dr Johnson refused to believe that it had been written by a woman, pronouncing that, 'Women can spin very well, but they cannot write a good cookery book'. Most manuscript cookery books, however, continued to be haphazardly arranged, with recipes simply being entered on the next available clean sheet or even wherever a space presented itself. As a rule, in the course of the eighteenth century, published recipe books show an increasing degree of organisation.

Frontispiece of Elizabeth Price, The New Universal and Complete Confectioner *(London, 1760), showing the mistress talking to her housekeeper. National Library of Scotland.*

While young ladies were expected to be skilled in the domestic arts and might be taught to cook and to keep house, even moderately wealthy households employed both a cook and a housekeeper (as had Lady Ochtertyre in the 1730s). Answering to the lady of the house, it was the housekeeper's role to assist her mistress in the day-to-day management of the house. This was an important position and vital to the smooth running of the household. In a large establishment, the mistress did not have the time, nor was she in a position to supervise all of the servants. Above all, it was not thought a suitable occupation for a lady.

In the course of the eighteenth century, manuals appeared which aimed to ensure the smooth functioning of the household. One such was that of Susanna Whatman who wrote that the mistress must 'depend upon her housekeeper to see all her orders are enforced and every rule kept up'.[10] As one of the few positions, apart from that of cook, in which a girl could hope to achieve any degree of social mobility, the job of housekeeper was highly sought after. Impoverished but educated girls, perhaps those who had attended the appropriate classes, aspired to these posts.

The housekeeper's role at about this time is vividly described in a small notebook entitled 'Rules to be observed by the housekeeper at Saltoun Hall and Instructions to her'.[11] Probably drawn up for the benefit of a new servant, the instructions note that 'when anything doubtful occurs . . . which is not found in the aforesaid Directions the housekeeper is to consult Mrs Fletcher thereupon and is not to give any heed to what the other servants say is the Custom of the family'.

Supplies of foodstuffs and supervision of the kitchen were but two aspects of the housekeeper's role. In respect of the former, Mrs Fletcher wrote, 'She is to have the Charge of the Larder and of the Raw Meat and Cold meat'. A degree of foresight was required, as the housekeeper was to consult with her mistress 'about whatever Provisions or other necessary Articles may be wanted before they be needed'. Furthermore, she was to oversee the cook and kitchen maid to ensure that 'no wrong use be made of any of the Articles'. Her duties did not stop there as 'every day [she was] to see Dinner Dish'd and sent properly to Table – She is to make the jellies and Blamonges. Silabubs etc'.

To return to the Erskine household, the housekeeper both in Argyle Square, Edinburgh, and at Alva, was Mary Dudgeon. As housekeeper, Mrs Dudgeon was

---

[9] In both Scotland and England most cookery writers were female; in France and Italy they tended to be men. The explanation probably lies in the more functional approach to cookery in Britain.

[10] Thomas Balston, ed., *The Housekeeping Book of Susanna Whatman, 1776-1800* (London, 1956).

[11] National Library of Scotland, Fletcher of Saltoun papers, MS.17080, ff.134-7.

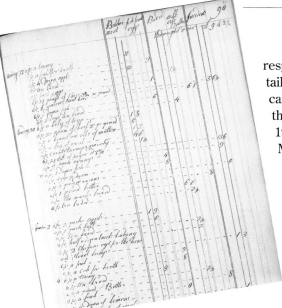

Mary Dudgeon's account book, 1752-1758.
Mrs Dudgeon's account book is a record of one household's expenditure, largely, but not entirely, on food.
National Library of Scotland, Adv.MS.2.1.9.

responsible for a good deal of daily expenditure, of which she kept detailed records.[12] At some point, her account book for 1752 to 1758 became separated from the Erskine family archive and was acquired by the Faculty of Advocates' Library in the late nineteenth century. In 1939, it was reunited with Lord Alva's archive when the Erskine-Murray papers came to the National Library of Scotland.[13]

Mrs Dudgeon's account book is a record of one household's expenditure, largely, but not entirely, on food. The book opens with records of the cash she received to 'lay out for the use of the family'. Most of this money came directly from Mrs Erskine, with a few payments 'from my Master'.[14] The extent of Mary Dudgeon's responsibility is indicated by the numerous entries for miscellaneous household expenses. These are varied and reflect the myriad day-to-day activities of the household. Fourpence was paid for 'the kitchen chimney sweeping'. Mrs Dudgeon also paid deliverymen – 'to a carter for caring hony from Pearth' – and bought such necessities as 'sope [soap] and starch blue for a bed washing 1sh 7d'.

Most of the accounts for foodstuffs are for raw ingredients. Once again, nowhere is the total number of people living in the house given. Save for rare occasions, the presence of guests, and the absence of family members, goes unrecorded. Many of these defects are supplied by the family papers, and within these limitations, the daily accounts build up a detailed picture of the eating habits of a vibrant, bustling, middle-class Edinburgh household.

Although Mrs Dudgeon rarely names her suppliers, by the 1750s Edinburgh boasted numerous retailers from whom she could have stocked the larders and store cupboards in the Argyle Square house.[15] Many of these tradesmen were general grocers whose shops boasted a wide range of foodstuffs and household goods. There were also specialist fleshers, poultrymen, fishmongers, fruiterers, ale sellers, and vintners.

Despite the growing number of shopkeepers, foodstuffs also continued to be sold on the streets by itinerant tradesmen. In his *Edinburgh Fugitive Pieces*, comparing Edinburgh in 1763, 1783 and 1793, William Creech wrote that 'Edinburgh was chiefly supplied with vegetables and garden stuff from Musselburgh and the neighbourhood, which were called through the streets by women with creels or baskets on their backs'.[16]

When the family was at their country home at Alva in Stirlingshire, the accounts are largely for eggs, fish, bread, and luxury items such as lemons and spices. In Edinburgh the picture changes, often dramatically. There, while Mrs Dudgeon bought goods from the grocer and baker, the emphasis is firmly on

[12] National Library of Scotland, Mary Dudgeon's Account Book, 1752-1758, Adv.MS.2.1.9.

[13] National Library of Scotland, Erskine-Murray papers, MSS.5070-138. The non-legal books and manuscripts in the Faculty of Advocates' Library were transferred to the nation in 1925 when the National Library of Scotland was created.

[14] Records of payments to Mary Dudgeon appear in James Erskine's account book, National Library of Scotland, Adv.MS.16.1.5.

[15] James Gilhooley, *A Directory of Edinburgh in 1752* (Edinburgh, 1988).

[16] William Creech, *Edinburgh Fugitive Pieces* (Edinburgh, 1815).

purchases of meat and fish. As city-dwellers, the Erskines did not have access to herds of cattle, flocks of sheep, and well-stocked hen-runs, from which to select their daily meat. Rather, Mrs Dudgeon bought butcher-meat as required.

The large amount of meat consumed is still striking: the diet of well-off Scots remained meat-dominated. Mutton, pork, and poultry all feature here, but it is the quantity of beef bought that stands out. In early January 1753 alone, no less than 16 lb of beef was bought on the second, 12 lb on the fourth, 21 lb on the sixth, another 21 lb on the ninth, and 30 lb on the sixteenth of the month.

Much of this beef probably went into the daily broth pot, still very much a staple of the Scots' diet. This is reflected in the amount of space given over to soups and broths in published Scottish recipe books. Elizabeth Cleland devotes the first chapter of her *New and Easy Method of Cookery* to a wide variety of 'Gravies, Soups, Broths and Pottages'. Traditional broths based on beef, mutton, poultry, game, and vegetables all appear. In addition, there are now numerous soups with such diverse ingredients as vermicelli, almonds, lobsters, and cucumbers. English cookery books of the time give far less prominence to soups: Hannah Glasse gives them a short chapter, and Eliza Smith discusses them only in the context of 'Broths, etc., for the Sick'.

Beef was also served as a traditional roast or boiled joint, or in a sauce. Mrs Cleland gives two recipes for the increasingly popular beef collops. The recipe shown here is for highly spiced, rolled collops, served in a wine and lemon sauce.

'The Head of the West Bow', from Walter Geikie, Studies from Nature Drawn and Etched *(Edinburgh, 1831).* Despite the growing numbers of shopkeepers, foodstuffs continued to be sold on the streets by itinerant tradesmen. *National Library of Scotland.*

TO MAKE BEEF COLLOPS

Cut thin slices of Beef where it is tender, and beat it well with your Rolling-pin; then season it with Pepper, Salt, Cloves, Mace, and sweet Herbs, and Lemon-peel very fine; season it with spice as above: Lay a Lair of this all over your Collops, and roll them up tight, put them in a can with a little Butter, cover them close and bake them; when they are done, take them out in Slices, and put them on a Dish, pour on some of their own Gravy, with a little white Wine and the juice of half a lemon: Dont make it sour; you may thicken it with a little Butter and Flour grate Nutmeg on it.

Poultry, particularly hens and chickens, was bought daily for the family in Argyle Square. Less frequently, Mrs Dudgeon bought ducks and geese, sometimes followed by a note of 'apples for a sauce for the goose'. Elizabeth Cleland gives a number of suggestions for cooking geese, including 'to dress a Goose with Onions or Cabage', 'To souse a Goose', and 'To boil a Goose'. Her roast goose was served with an apple sauce and, optionally, stuffed with apples or potatoes.

TO ROAST A GOOSE

Stuff it with boiled Potatoes, and Onions, chopped small, seasoned with Pepper and Salt, or, you may stuff it with Apples, or roast it without any Stuffing; but season it high, and roast it an Hour and a Quarter. Put Gravy in the Dish, and Apple Sauce in a bowl.

Living so close to the east coast and the fishing villages of East Lothian and Fife, it is hardly surprising that fish was high on Mrs Dudgeon's shopping list. While there were fishmongers in Edinburgh in the 1750s, numerous fishwives from nearby Musselburgh and Prestonpans carried baskets of fish on their backs into the city and sold their fish in the streets.

Fresh fish was bought for the Erskine family several times a week. Often, the entries are disappointingly brief stating no more than 'To a dozen of fish'. Others are more specific, and cod, whiting, haddock, herring, flounders, and the occasional salmon were all bought. Mrs Dudgeon usually paid sixpence for half a dozen herrings. Haddock cost threepence half-penny for twelve, and on 24 November 1754 '20 fish haddoes [haddock] and whiting' cost sixpence. Considering that a leg of mutton could cost two shillings and sixpence, and half a dozen eggs tuppence, fish was relatively cheap.

Elizabeth Cleland's cookery book features a lengthy chapter on fish cookery: 'On dressing all kinds of FISH, and their sauces'. Her recipes range from potted herring to stewed haddock, and flat fish in jelly to fried whiting. Salmon merited several recipes, and could be variously broiled, pickled, hashed, farced, fried, or pickled.

Mrs Cleland suggested stewing haddock. The fish were first boiled in water with onion, seasonings, lemon-peel and parsley. When cooked, a little wine was added, the fish was removed and the sauce thickened using beaten egg yolks (the same thickener as used at Ochtertyre in the 1730s). Mrs Cleland's final sentence may have been aimed at the pupils in her cookery school as it takes the form of a word of warning to the unwary not to allow the mixture to curdle, and to stir until well-blended after adding the butter and flour.

'Bargaining for fish', from Walter Geikie, Studies from Nature Drawn and Etched *(Edinburgh, 1831).*
National Library of Scotland.

TO STEW HADDOCKS OR WHITING

Put them in a Pan, with a little Water, Pepper, Salt, Mace, chopped Parsley, Lemon-Peel, and Onion, a good piece of Butter worked in Flour; let them boil in a quick fire. When you think they are enough, put in a little Wine, then take out the Fish, and thicken the sauce with the Yolks of three Eggs well beaten; take care it does not curdle: When you put Butter and Flour in any Thing; stir it until it dissolves; shred the Parsley.

During the winter months, the Erskine household ate large amounts of shell-fish, particularly lobsters, oysters, and crabs. On 13 November 1754, Mrs Dudgeon paid eight shillings for two barrels of pickled oysters. Later that month she bought two lobsters for one shilling. On another occasion, two lobsters and a hundred oysters cost six shillings. The most usual way to eat shell-fish was to cook them in a brine of water and salt and then eat them cold, but a wide range of cooking methods for shell-fish were known.

Mrs Cleland's suggestions for lobster include lobster soup, scalloped lobster, fried lobster, lobster sauce, and 'lobster the Italian way'. This last dish consisted of boiled lobster flesh in a sauce of white wine, truffles, mushrooms, lemon juice, sweet herbs, and spices. Just as dishes combining fish and meat were becoming popular, so a number of her recipes call for more than one type of shell-fish. As Mrs Dudgeon often bought oysters and lobsters on the same day, it is possible that the Erskine family ate such combinations.

The popularity and remarkable versatility of oysters continued. Mrs Cleland gives recipes for oyster soup, pickled oysters, scalloped oysters, and even fricasseed oysters. As well as being dishes in their own right, oysters could be added to almost any savoury. Among Mrs Cleland's fish dishes alone, hashed salmon included minced shrimps and oysters, and fried salmon, roasted cod's head and baked turbot were all served with an oyster sauce. Also, oysters appear throughout the savoury sections of her book: they were boiled, as in 'Turkey with celery'; chickens and ducks were farced with oysters; and they were added to the sauces for stewed pigeons and minced hare.

When the Erskine family was in Edinburgh, scarcely a day passed on which Mrs Dudgeon did not buy fresh vegetables. Sometimes, there is a general entry for 'gardin things', but more often than not specific vegetables are noted. A large variety was bought, among the most popular being turnips, carrots, savoys, potatoes, celery, broccoli, spinach, radishes, peas, cauliflowers, and onions in season. The 1854 Ordnance Survey map of Edinburgh shows that Argyle Square had a central pleasure-garden, but no kitchen gardens – hence the need to purchase vegetables.

Unfortunately, the quantities of vegetables bought are not often given. The entry for 10 December 1752 is typical: 'To greens, turnips, potatoes and carets [carrots] . . . 6½d'. There were a few exceptions: peas were bought by the pound or the peck; asparagus by the half hundred, or more often by the hundred. Asparagus seems to have been a favourite dish as, when in season in May 1753, it was bought almost every other day.

On at least two occasions payments were made 'to the Alloa corier [courier] for bringing cucumbers from Alva'. As cucumbers were expensive to transport and almost certainly available in Edinburgh, sentimental reasons probably lay behind this operation. Possibly the cucumbers were eaten raw as part of a salad, but it is tempting to think Margaret Erskine knew of Mrs Cleland's recipe for stuffed cucumbers. Here, flour is used as a thickening agent.

A RAGOO OF STUFFED CUCUMBERS

Take as many Cucumbers as will fill your Dish, pare them, and scoop out the Seeds, blanch them with boiling Water, then put them in cold Water, stuff them with Veal, Beef, and Sewet [suet] shred very small; season it with Pepper, Salt, Onions, Lemon-peel and spice. Thicken it with Butter and Flour.

Potatoes were bought at least twice a week and must have appeared on the table regularly. As at Ochtertyre, it is unlikely that they were simply boiled and eaten as a standard accompaniment to a meal. Mrs Cleland's recipe book indicates the range of possibilities being explored in the mid-1750s. Potato cheesecakes called for boiled, peeled potatoes mixed with beaten eggs, sugar, lemon-peel and orange-peel, nutmeg, and a glass of brandy, all baked together with a pastry base. A potato pudding was made in much the same way but with the addition of melted butter and a puff-pastry case. Another mixture made potato fritters when dropped by the spoonful into a pan of boiling oil. Potatoes were still considered something of a delicacy with their role undetermined between the sweet and the savoury.

No doubt a large proportion of the vegetables bought by Mrs Dudgeon found their way into the broth-pot. Of the rest, some would be served as accompaniments to meat-based dishes. Elizabeth Cleland gives recipes for 'chickens with Tongues, Colliflowers and Greens', 'boil[ed] chickens and Asparagus'. Mrs Cleland does give a few recipes for vegetable dishes, but, as is usual for the period, she has no separate vegetable section: rather, vegetable recipes are scattered throughout her work, indicating their relative lack of importance.

'Milk and yerning [rennet] to make cheesecakes' was bought frequently for the Erskine household. These tarts, filled with curds, eggs, spices and possibly currants, evolved out of the spiced cheese tarts of the Middle Ages. Most British recipe books of the early eighteenth century include recipes for cheesecakes. Some add rennet, while others rely simply on boiling the milk to separate the curds and whey.

Elizabeth Cleland's recipe for cheesecakes is a typically Scottish unrenneted version. First, cream, milk, and eggs were beaten together; the mixture was then placed on the fire until it separated, when the whey could be drained off. Nutmeg, cinnamon, rosewater, Malaga wine, sugar, butter, crushed biscuits, and finally currants were added. Mrs Cleland concludes, 'You may bake them in any shape of Crust you please'.

In the mid-eighteenth century, cheesecakes were evolving rapidly, and several different dishes were known by the name, some containing neither cheese nor curds. C. Anne Wilson describes these as 'custardy mixtures of eggs, butter, flour, and unrenneted cream, sweetened and spiced'.[17] Later, they were flavoured with sharp fruits such as lemons and oranges. Savoury cheesecakes were also popular. Elizabeth Cleland added Malaga wine or brandy to her cheesecakes, and Mrs Johnston's were fortified with brandy. Curiously, alcohol in cheesecakes is a feature of Scottish and not English recipe books.

With several different dishes known by the same name, cookery books tended to carry more than one cheesecake recipe: Elizabeth Cleland alone has recipes for cheesecakes of oranges, almonds, eggs, and potatoes. Orange cheesecake was made using the skins of two Seville oranges 'boiled in four or five Waters, til all the Bitterness is off them, and the skin is so tender you may thrust a Straw in them'. The skins were then pounded to a paste with fine sugar, and beaten eggs, butter, and a little brandy added. Cleland writes: 'Put Paste in the Patty-pans, and half fill them; half an Hour bakes them in a slow Oven'.

[17] C. Anne Wilson, *Food and Drink in Britain* (London, 1973), p. 157.

Lemon cheesecakes were made to the same recipe as the orange version but without the need to change the boiling water. The resulting dish resembled what we know today as lemon cheese or lemon curd. Almond cheesecakes were based on blanched almonds pounded to a paste in brandy or rosewater. Mrs Cleland's egg cheesecake consisted of beaten eggs thickened with flour. More eggs were then beaten with cream and butter, heated over a fire, and the egg and flour mixture added when it had thickened but not boiled. Half a pound of currants was added, and the mixture seasoned with sugar, salt, lemon-peel and nutmeg.

The quantity of sugar bought by Mrs Dudgeon, and the number of sweetened desserts, cakes, biscuits, pastries, and creams in Mrs Cleland's recipe book, indicate the extent to which sugar had entered the diet. Although still retaining its earlier roles as condiment, sweetener, and medicine (see pages 11 and 18), as sugar became more readily available with the opening up of the West Indian sugar estates it rapidly became an integral part of Scottish cookery, its use no longer confined to the wealthiest members of society. In the course of a single century the British diet had changed from being starch-based to sugar-based.[18]

In September 1753, Mrs Dudgeon twice bought three lemons at a penny each 'for Mr Maguire's jelly', and once bought four calves' feet for the same purpose. The only references to Mr Maguire occur between 10 and 25 September 1753. Save for a tart bought for him on 25 September, all the references are to jellies. Mr Maguire was probably Margaret Erskine's father, Hugh, who died in November 1753. Concerned for her father during his last illness, his daughter ordered a series of nourishing jellies for him.

Jellies, made from calves' feet, and flavoured with almonds and spices, were an established feature of medieval feasts. Later, both meat jellies and sweet 'pudding' jellies were known. Although they remained dishes for special occasions, jellies formed an important part of the sizeable repertoire of dishes emerging to tempt the jaded appetites of the sick and delicate.

From the seventeenth century, jellies were sometimes sweetened with sugar and flavoured with rosewater and spices. Later, these flavourings were largely replaced by lemon juice. Coloured jellies were popular in Georgian times: Mr Maguire's jelly may have been coloured red using cochineal. Alternatives were syrup of violets, which gave a blue colour, saffron for yellow, and spinach for green. Sometimes, a jelly with a striped effect, known as a 'ribbon-jelly', was produced using a range of colours.

'Jellies' from Isabella Beeton, The Book of Household Management (London, 1869). *National Library of Scotland.*

[18] Mintz, p. 14.

Jellies could be stiffened using hartshorn (originally made from the shavings of harts' horns), isinglass (obtained from the bladders of certain fresh-water fish, particularly sturgeon), or, more traditionally, calves' feet. Elizabeth Cleland gives recipes for both hartshorn and calves' feet jellies. In the latter case, stiffening was assisted by 'a quarter of a pound of Hartshorn, or Two-Pence worth of Isinglass'. After boiling 'til they are all in Tatters', the cooled stock was skimmed and strained. Cleland concludes: 'the best way to season Jelly is to your Taste, but you may put a Mutchkin of Wine and four Lemons to three Mutchkins of Stock; season it with Cinnamon, Sugar and the rind of a Lemon; clear it as you do the Hartshorn Jelly, with whites of Eggs'. To clear jelly, beaten egg whites were whisked into the mixture, which was then boiled for 15 minutes. The jelly was then sieved through a fine cloth until clear. As well as adding to the flavour, white wine gave an amber colour.

In sharp contrast to Mrs Dudgeon's daily purchases of vegetables are the all too infrequent references to fruit. There are occasional entries for apples, often bought for a sauce to accompany roast goose. For a short time in June, strawberries were bought several times a week at one shilling a pint or sometimes they were sent down from Alva. Fresh cream was often bought at the same time (a chopin of sweet cream cost eight pence), perhaps to serve with the strawberries. In his description of Edinburgh in 1763, William Creech notes that 'there are immense quantities of strawberries sold in the Edinburgh market during the short period that they continue. They are sold, upon average, at 6d the Scots pint,

*'Apples 5 a ha'penny',
from Walter Geikie,*
Studies from Nature
Drawn and Etched
*(Edinburgh, 1831).
National Library of
Scotland.*

apples 5 a ha'penny

equal to four English pints, and without any stem or husk, as in other places. It is estimated that 100,000 Scots, or 400,000 English pints, are annually sold in favourable seasons, in the city and in the suburbs, value L.2500'.[19]

Sometimes, seasonal soft fruit was bought specifically for preserving. In July 1754, Mrs Dudgeon spent two shillings and sixpence on '12 pints of curran berrys for Jelly' and '12 Jelly pots for ditto'. This was probably redcurrant jelly, now replacing spiced sauces as an accompaniment for meat. The following month, blackberries, gooseberries, cherries, raspberries, and apricots were purchased 'for jelly'.

An entry in James Erskine's personal account book for rent for an orchard suggests that the family had their own source of fruit. Presumably, the produce of this unidentified orchard met most of the requirements of the household when in Edinburgh. No doubt, supplies of preserves as well as fruit reached Argyle Square from the family seat at Alva.

TO BAKE APPLES

Put your Apples in an Earthen Can, with a few Cloves, a little Lemon-peel, coarse Sugar, and a Glass of red Wine; cover them closs [close]; they will take an Hour's baking in a quick Oven. You may do Pears the same Way, but they will take two Hour's baking.

In mid-eighteenth century Scotland, fruit was still looked upon with some suspicion as a potentially dangerous foodstuff, and eating raw fruit was discouraged. Elizabeth Cleland gives a few recipes for fruit-based desserts, such as baked apples (shown here) and fruit tarts. She also includes the fruit cakes favoured earlier at Dunrobin and Saltoun. Fruit, however, did not yet feature daily on the Scots table. As at Dunrobin and elsewhere, it was still traditionally collected by the lady of the house and her maids, and preserved in large quantities of sugar to provide delicacies for the coming winter months.

Mrs Dudgeon paid a weekly bread bill, and must have had an account with a local baker. The family's basic order for bread was fairly constant, costing sixpence per week. Speciality breads such as 'bread for breakfast', 'french rols' (bought by the dozen), and 'tea bread' appear less frequently, possibly when visitors were present. Sometimes the baker's bill includes apple tarts and cakes. Bread warrants a separate column in Mrs Dudgeon's accounts, indicating its importance in the diet.

The type of bread eaten in this wealthy household is not specified, but at least a large proportion of it was probably wheaten. In southern England, consumption of wheaten bread was widespread, and in the north barley bread was common. However, in Europe, rye bread was the norm in Germany, the Low Countries, Denmark, and France.

Although ordinary Scots continued to eat oatmeal and bread made from rye, by the 1750s the habit of eating wheaten bread was spreading, especially in the towns. This was due at least in part to the agricultural improvements of the eighteenth century and to improved trading communications. Nevertheless, the change to wheaten bread was a slow process, as Ramsay of Ochtertyre indicated when he wrote in 1760 that 'within the last 39 years, little wheat bread was eaten in private

[19] Creech, p. 94.

gentleman's families, unless at breakfast. Indeed, at dinner and supper a few slices were cut for strangers and laid atop of the cakes which last were generally preferred'.

Belonging to the country's legal élite, James and Margaret Erskine were among the first to leave Edinburgh's Old Town for the new, spacious town-houses set in leafy Argyle Square, one of the earliest phases of the town's eighteenth-century development. While retaining ties with their ancestral home at Alva, the family was anxious to appear in the vanguard of fashion. The purchases made by the housekeeper, Mrs Dudgeon, reflect this concern. Similarly, Lady Alva's sister, Jacobina, came to Edinburgh to attend classes at the new schools for girls. Cookery schools, such as that run by Elizabeth Cleland, and the book of recipes intended for her pupils, ensured that educated, forward-looking Scots were aware of recent developments in the culinary sphere.

38

Spring fruit Pudding

Peel & wash 3 or 4 dozen sticks of Rhubarb, put it in a
stew pan with the peel of a lemon a bit of Cinnamon
two cloves and as much moist sugar as will sweeten
it well, if over a fire and reduce it to a marmalade,
pass it through a hair sieve, then add the peel of a lemon
& half an nutmeg grated & 1/2 good butter & the yolks
& 1 eggs & one whole mix it well together and bake in a
dish that will not contain it well good puff paste
half the mixture in and bake it half an hour.

Spring fruit soup

Clean an about 4 dozen sticks of Rhubarb blanch it
in water 3 or 4 minutes drain it on a sieve & put it
in a stew pan with 2 Onions sliced, a Carrot on 3
of lean ham & a good bit of butter let it stew gently
over a slow fire till tender then put in 2 quarts of
good consommé to which add 2 or 3 ounces of bread
crumbs, boil 15 minutes skim off all the fat season with
salt & Cayenne Pepper pass it through a tammis &
serve up with fried bread

6 TRIFLE, CURRY AND RHUBARB

BURNFOOT, 1782-1813

Diary of Stephana Malcolm, September 1813.
Revolving around meals and visits, Stephana Malcolm's diary centres on the social engagements which formed the daily routine of this unmarried, leisured, young lady of good family.
National Library of Scotland, Acc.6684/40.

'6 [SEPTEMBER 1813] MRS WM OLIVER AND MRS MALCOLM CAME TO BREAKFAST MEANING to return home that night but the rain prevented them. Mr Edward armstrong came to dinner . . . 21 [September 1813] we were alone until the afternoon when Mrs Elliot from Langholm and Miss Moncrieff came to tea they staid all night.'[1] Revolving around meals and visits to and from friends and neighbours, Stephana Malcolm's diary for 1813 centres on the social engagements which formed the daily routine of this unmarried, leisured, young lady of good family.

Situated near Langholm in Dumfriesshire in south-western Scotland, the 'small but beautiful estate of Burnfoot' was home to George Malcolm and his family. 'A man of very superior character and attainments, [George Malcolm] was an excellent classical scholar and of exemplary Piety and Virtue. He resided at Burnfoot throughout life, and not only farmed that small place but speculated in others with no better success, I fear, than usually attends men who attempt the management of concerns for which they are not fitted.'[2] In short, George Malcolm was no farmer.

Stephana Malcolm in old age, c.1860.
As the unmarried daughter of George Malcolm of Burnfoot, Stephana Malcolm had 'every advantage except fortune'.
By permission of Mrs Angela Kellie.

[1] National Library of Scotland, Malcolm of Burnfoot papers, Acc.6684/40.
[2] National Library of Scotland, Malcolm of Burnfoot papers, Acc.6684/28.

While none too successful in his business affairs, George Malcolm married Margaret Pasley, the daughter of a neighbouring laird, and produced a large family of ten sons and seven daughters. It was said of their children that 'they had every advantage except fortune'. Margaret Pasley's English connections resulted in most of their sons being educated south of the Border, and the family made frequent visits to their English relations.

Burnfoot House from the east.
By permission of Mrs Angela Kellie.

Over the years, the family fortunes were considerably depleted by what has been termed George Malcolm's 'untoward speculation'. Consequently, in common with many another landed, but none-too-wealthy, Scottish family the sons were sent out into the world to fend for themselves, where they acquitted themselves commendably in the public service: Sir John Malcolm became Governor of Bombay; Sir Pulteney Malcolm rose to become an Admiral, serving with distinction in the Napoleonic Wars; and their younger brother, Sir Charles Malcolm, became a Vice-Admiral.

Letters home, particularly from Sir Pulteney Malcolm, survive among the family papers. Most of his letters are addressed to his wife, Clementina, and his unmarried sisters, Wilhelmina and Stephana Malcolm. Few replies from Burnfoot or Douglen (another family property) have survived. However, the Malcolm women have left a remarkable record in a series of cookery books covering four generations and over a hundred years.[3]

The first of these notebooks was begun in 1782 by Margaret Malcolm, wife of George. In turn her daughter, Stephana, kept three cookery books, of which two were begun in 1790 and 1791, when she was a young woman, and the third towards the end of her long life in the mid-nineteenth century. Stephana's sister-in-law, Clementina, started her recipe book in 1812, soon after her marriage. Clementina's granddaughter, Mary Douglas Malcolm, kept her recipe books in the 1870s and 1890s. Many of the recipes are common to more than one author, but the arrival of new dishes and cooking methods distinguishes the generations.

[3] National Library of Scotland, Malcolm of Burnfoot papers, Acc.10708. All the recipes featured in this chapter are taken from this series of cookery books, and in particular those of Stephana Malcolm.

Taken together, the seven recipe books provide a valuable insight into the eating habits of one of the most notable families of south-west Scotland.

George Malcolm's wife, Margaret, was a local girl, from the village of Craig, near Langholm. They married in 1761, but the first entries in Margaret's recipe book date from 1782. This was very much a working notebook, in which entries were made over a number of years. Margaret died in 1811, but, as was the case with Lady Saltoun's recipe books over a century earlier, the volume remained in use, the store of recipes being added to by her grandson's wife, Charlotte Elizabeth Malcolm, until the late nineteenth century. Intended for personal and family use, none of the entries is signed. However, some of the recipes are dated, and in some cases sources are given.

Lady Grace Douglas, wife of George Douglas of Cavers, was the source of the recipes for 'Dressed Pease', 'Lobster Sauce', and 'Orange Jelly'. Given that Margaret Malcolm and Lady Grace were related by marriage, this is perhaps not surprising. There are also recipes given to Margaret Malcolm by female members of several other local families including Lady Carnegie and Mrs Wilson from Cavers. These same women are frequently mentioned in Stephana Malcolm's diary. Doubtless, exchanges of favourite recipes as well as gossip took place at their gatherings.

Silver tea service from Hopetoun House, c.1735. National Museums of Scotland.

While men were present at many of Stephana Malcolm's social engagements, many of the afternoon meetings were largely, if not entirely, female. Ostensibly, the women met to 'drink tea', still as much a ceremony as at Saltoun in Margaret Carnegie's time. Since the repeal of the tea taxes in 1784 and their replacement by a flat, lower rate of duty, tea-drinking had become more affordable, and its popularity had spread. By the end of the eighteenth century, even farmers' wives gathered in the afternoon for what had become known as the 'four hours', the forerunner of afternoon tea.

To accompany the beverage, rich tea breads and biscuits were now served. This recipe for tea-bread appears in Margaret Malcolm's cookery book.

FOR TEA BREAD
Rub 3lbs of flour into one lb of butter, four eggs beat up, $\frac{1}{2}$ a lb of sugar, six spoonfuls of yeast and a quarter of an ounce of carraway seeds. Form into cakes & bake.

Groups of women meeting in one another's houses to drink tea may seem innocuous enough today, but at the time the 'four hours' was regarded with suspicion. Duncan Forbes of Culloden denounced tea-drinking as the root of all ills in Scottish society, and ministers and doctors were particularly vocal in their disapproval.

In his account of Ayrshire village life in his *Annals of the Parish*, John Galt has Mr Balwhidder bemoan that 'before this year [1761], the drinking of tea was little known in the parish . . . but now it became very rife'. Subterfuge was necessary to indulge, and he writes that 'the commoner sort did not let it be known they were taking to the new luxury, especially the elderly women who, for that reason, had their ploys in out-houses and by-places'. By 1813, the Malcolm women did not need to resort to such devices: they drank tea openly, sometimes inviting their men-folk to join them. It was only when men began to be included that the vehement protests about these so-called dangerous gatherings ceased.

The eighteenth-century woman did not consider the provision of food in isolation from other housewifely duties. This is reflected in the cookery books of the time. Recipes for fruit wines, such as gooseberry, currant, and parsnip wine, are sprinkled throughout the Malcolm of Burnfoot recipe books. Similarly, beverages such as light ginger beer, ginger pop, champagne, posset, and even an exotic sounding drink by the name of 'Nanzean de Martinique' appear alongside the 'stewed brisket of beef' and 'savoury potatoes'.

In time-honoured tradition, medicinal and household recipes are interspersed with culinary 'receipts'. So, hints on the best way 'to clean and polish grates' appear next to 'dripping to keep good', and this in turn is followed by the reminder that 'wild mint will keep off mice or rats and tansy at the bed head will keep away bugs and fleas'. The principal purpose of all the Malcolm family's recipe books, however, was to record methods of preparing and preserving foodstuffs.

Preserving, particularly of fruit and vegetables, was a skill expected of gently-born women. Consequently, it occupies a disproportionate position in their recipe books compared with its importance in the diet. Nevertheless, Stephana Malcolm's recipe books show a noticeable change in emphasis even compared with Mrs Cleland's work. Up to at least the mid-eighteenth century, there was a concentration on methods of preservation, and particularly on jams, jellies, and marmalades. While such recipes do appear here, they are generally more imaginative.

Recipes for fruit pastes of red and green gooseberries and 'common plumbs' are remarkably similar to those made at Dunrobin in 1683. Stephana recommends they be 'put into shapes of cups or bowls, which makes it a pretty ready dish to turn out when required without prepa-

Tea caddy, with separate containers for green, bohea and mixed teas, 1725 and 1767. National Museums of Scotland.

ration'. There are two recipes for marmalade: 'marmalade' and 'marmalade in a hurry'. Interestingly, marmalade now means orange marmalade, the other fruit versions having largely been dropped. In the place of the fruit 'cakes', jams and jellies so popular at Dunrobin and Saltoun in the late seventeenth century are fruit wines and a wide range of hot and cold puddings.

There are custards, creams, and fruit tarts as before, but also a far greater variety of desserts, such as bread and butter pudding, treacle pudding, plum pudding, and muffin pudding. Stephana Malcolm probably only noted recipes that were new, that her friends had recommended, or that were of particular interest to her: there would be no need to write down tried-and-tested recipes in everyday use.

Stephana's fruit-based desserts are largely for orchard produce. So, recipes for home-grown fruits, notably gooseberries, apples, pears, redcurrants, and blackcurrants predominate. The more exotic fruits, such as apricots and quinces, and imported lemons and oranges, do not warrant as many recipes as they did a century earlier. The preserves and delicacies made by the ladies of the Earl of Sutherland's household had a dual purpose: practically, they were a means of conserving superfluous produce; symbolically, they were intended to impress. Stephana's recipes were of a practical nature.

Among the numerous apple-based recipes are 'Apple Ginger', 'Mother Eve's Pudding', and 'Apple Charlotte', the latter traditionally named after George III's Queen Charlotte. The highly-spiced 'Apple Ginger' was a delicacy stored in jelly pots and 'tied down like other sweetmeats'. No less than ½ lb of rough ginger and 1 oz of 'pounded ginger' was added to the 12 lb of apples (preferably Paradise Pippins). The recipe for Apple Charlotte consists of stewed apples mixed with lemon juice, cloves, nutmeg, and sugar, all baked in a mould lined with thin slices of bread. That for Mother Eve's Pudding is written amusingly in verse, but the method is assumed.

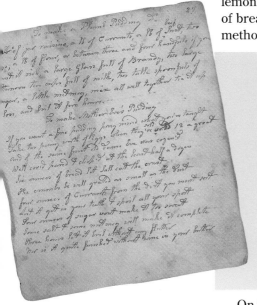

'Mother Eve's Pudding' and 'Plumb Pudding', in Stephana Malcolm's recipe book, begun in 1790.
In addition to the custards, creams, and fruit tarts present in earlier compilations, Stephana Malcolm's recipe books include a wide variety of fruit-based desserts.
National Library of Scotland, Acc.10708/2.

To make Mother Eve's Pudding

If you want a fine pudding pray mind what you're taught
Take two penny worth of Eggs when they're sold 12 a groat
and of the same fruit old dame Eve was cozen'd
Well cor'd pared and chop'd at the least half a dozen
Six ounces of bread let Sall eat the crust
The crumbs be well gratted as small as the dust
four ounces of Currants from the dirt you must sort
Lest it get in your teeth and spoil all your sport
Four ounces of sugar wont make it too sweet
Some salt & some nutmeg will make it complete
Three hours let it boil without any fluther
Nor is it quite finished without wine in your brother.

On the same opening as 'Mother Eve's Pudding', Stephana gives her recipe for a rich plum pudding with large quantities of dried fruits. Associated with Christmas from the early eighteenth century, plum puddings have their origins in medieval pottages or porridges of stewed meat and dried fruits. Stephana's plum pudding was laced with alcohol, and so could be prepared well in advance and stored away until required.

TO MAKE A PLUMB PUDDING

a lb of jar raisins, a lb of Currants, a lb of beef Suett, two Eggs, a lb of flour, or between three and four handfuls if you want it rich, a large Glass full of Brandy, two large afternoon tea cups full of milk, two table spoonfuls of sugar, a little nut-meg, mix all well together tie it up closs [close] and boil it five hours.

As in most Scottish cookery books of the time, soups and broths are important. Traditional recipes for pease soup, onion soup, giblet soup, white and brown soup are all present, but Stephana also had an eye for the novel: her imagination seems to have been caught by a recipe for 'Spring Fruit Soup'.[4] Sticks of rhubarb were sweated gently in butter with sliced onions, a carrot, and an ounce of lean ham. Two quarts of 'good consomme' were added, and the soup thickened with breadcrumbs and seasoned with cayenne pepper, before being sieved through a 'tammis' (fine sieve) and served with a helping of croutons.

SPRING FRUIT SOUP

clean as above [peel and wash] 4 dozen sticks of Rhubarb, blanch it in water 3 or 4 minutes drain it on a sieve & put it in a stew-pan with two Onions sliced, a Carrot, an oz of lean ham & a good bit of butter let it stew gently over a slow fire till tender then put in 2 quarts of good consomme to which add 2 or 3 ounces of bread-crumbs, boil 15 minutes skim off all the fat season with salt and Cayenne Pepper pass it through a tammis & serve up with fried bread.

This recipe for 'Spring Fruit Soup' is one of no fewer than three rhubarb recipes. 'Spring Fruit Pudding' is another of the numerous hot-pudding recipes. This time, the rhubarb was stewed with lemon-peel, cinnamon, cloves, and sugar until reduced 'to a marmalade'. The resulting mixture was sieved and more lemon-peel, nutmeg, butter, and eggs added. Then, Stephana instructs, 'have a pie dish that will just contain it with good puff paste put the mixture in and bake it half an hour'.

Stephana's third rhubarb recipe is for 'Spring cream or mock Gooseberry Fool'. This cold dessert was prepared in the same way as the pudding, but a pint of cream was added once the fruit had been stewed. The fool could be served up at once in glasses. Alternatively, 'if wanted in a shape', the instructions were to add 2 oz of isin-glass dissolved in a little water, strain, and add the cream. The mixture was then poured into a jelly mould and left to set.

These three rhubarb recipes appear, along with yet two more, in the 1823 edition of Dr Kitchiner's *The Cook's Oracle*. As an enthusiast for gastronomic purges, the medicinal qualities of rhubarb, as well as its value as a food, appealed to him.

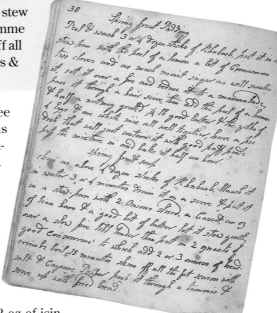

'Spring Fruit Pudding' and Spring Fruit Soup', from Stephana Malcolm's recipe book, begun in 1791. Stephana Malcolm includes no fewer than three rhubarb recipes in her cookery books. While the medicinal properties of rhubarb had been known for some time, its use as a foodstuff was still experimental. Stephana's third rhubarb recipe is for 'Spring Cream or mock Gooseberry fool'. *National Library of Scotland, Acc.10708/3.*

---

[4] In 1755, Mrs Cleland's 'Spring Soup' was made from lettuce, cucumber, and peas.

Stephana's recipes apparently pre-date Dr Kitchiner's work, but they may both have had the same source. Meg Dods includes 'Spring Fruit Soup' of 'gourds, peeled rhubarb, &c' in her *Cook and Housewife's Manual* of 1826. However, both the ingredients and method are different , suggesting that she had another source. The use of rhubarb stalks as a food was better known in northern Europe, and it may be that these recipes reached Britain from either Denmark or Germany.

Medicinal rhubarb from China, grown for its roots, was known in Britain from the time of the Romans. By the sixteenth century it was grown in the herb gardens of the wealthy. In 1721, the Laird of Saltoun paid five shillings to a Dr Maitland in Haddington for 'one ounce of the best rhubarb'.[5] Further north, the Duke of Atholl had a plantation of Turkey rhubarb at Blair Atholl in the 1770s. He sold the roots of his plants to an Edinburgh druggist.

The culinary use of rhubarb in which its stalks were eaten as a fruit came much later than the well-chronicled medicinal uses. Stephana Malcolm's rhubarb recipes are of some significance, being among the earliest known recipes for rhubarb as a food.[6] That the three very different recipes appear together suggests that Stephana considered it a curiosity. As a relatively new fruit, the treatment of rhubarb was still at an exploratory stage. Although the pudding recipe and the fool or cream are uses to which rhubarb might still be put today, the same cannot be said of 'Spring Fruit Soup'.

Other new foods, this time from the East, are in evidence in the Malcolm family's recipe books, including several curries, chutneys, and spicy ketchups. Stephana's brothers were no strangers to India – three of them died there – and they may well have been responsible for introducing Indian cookery to Burnfoot. However, such dishes are not peculiar to these recipe books, and the influence of the East is apparent in most cookery books of the time.

While George Malcolm's sons earned their living abroad, his daughters travelled for pleasure. Stephana Malcolm's diary for 1813 records a tour in England when she visited Plymouth and London before returning to Dumfriesshire via Birmingham and Carlisle. This experience is reflected in her recipe books. Stephana may have been introduced to 'Brown Windsor Soup' and 'Todenham Curry' when on a visit to Todenham in Gloucestershire, where her brother, Gilbert, was Rector.

The original Indian curries were intended as sauces to pour over and give piquancy to bland dishes such as rice. They were used in moderation, almost as a relish, and did not swamp the food. Among the several different curries known, some resembled a spicy stew based on fish, meat, or vegetables, while others were dry. The first curries to reach Europe appear in the seventeenth-century Portuguese recipe book *Arte de Cozinha*. Neither Elizabeth Cleland in 1755 nor Hannah Glasse in 1747 mention curry sauces, and it is not until the late eighteenth century that they begin to appear in the British culinary repertoire.

Ready-mixed curry powder was on sale in Britain from the 1780s. Living in remote Dumfriesshire, Stephana may have found it difficult to obtain, or perhaps she simply preferred to make her own. Whatever the reason, she includes five

[5] National Library of Scotland, Fletcher of Saltoun papers, MS.16855, f.76.
[6] Hannah Glasse includes a recipe for rhubarb tarts in *The Complete Confectioner* (London, 1760). She notes 'these tarts may be thought very odd, but they are very fine ones and have a pretty flavour'.

'Currie Powder', from Stephana Malcolm's recipe book, begun in 1791.
Ready-made curry powder was on sale in Britain from the 1780s but may have been difficult to obtain in remote Dumfriesshire, or perhaps Stephana Malcolm preferred to make her own. Stephana's curry powder recipes appear alongside suggestions for curried dishes, mostly based on poultry.
National Library of Scotland, Acc.10708/3.

recipes for curry powder, one of which made sufficient for twenty curries. Intended to supply the family's needs for some time, the powder was to be stored dry in a tin canister.

Stephana's recipes for curry powder differ considerably from each other, indicating a knowledge of a wide range of spices. The simplest version calls for turmeric, coriander, cumin, fenugreek and cayenne pepper 'all to be finely powdered well mixed and sifted'. Other spices mentioned include black pepper, ginger, cardamoms, cinnamon root, mace, powdered cassia, cloves, and allspice.

The curry powder recipes appear alongside curried dishes mostly based on poultry: at Burnfoot, curry was largely associated with chicken. The 'Gillsland receipt for Currie' calls for 'a nice fowl skinned', and the 'Curry Brighton' includes chicken pieces. 'Currie Topperfield' is yet another chicken curry recipe. However, Sir Archibald Campbell's 'Method of preparing an East India Curry' was for 'fowl, duck, rabbit, meat, fish or vegetables' combined with apples and onions and, of course, a tablespoonful of curry powder.

In its turn, chicken curry is followed by 'Chutney to eat with curry'. This consisted of a finely chopped 'sharp juicy apple' and an onion seasoned with vinegar and cayenne pepper. When apples were not available, green gooseberries could be substituted.

CURRIE TOPPERFIELD

Boil a chicken gently in a Pint of water with a little salt for 10 minutes, take a head of Garlick, a large onion sliced, and fry them with the chicken when cut up in butter for 5 minutes, put the chicken & into the liquor it was first boiled in, a table spoonful of Curry Powder, some Apples or pickled Cucumbers answer the purpose, stew these ingredients and the Chickens very gently till the sauce is about the thickness of cream, add a bit of butter rolled in flour if it is not thick enough to please.

Soup tureen and ladle, William Davie, Edinburgh, 1789-90. Huntly House Museum, Edinburgh.

Recipes for 'mulgatawy' (mulligatawny) soup also appear. Made in much the same way as the chicken curry, mutton or veal stock replaces the water as a cooking liquid, and the whole chicken is simply stewed until it falls to pieces.[7] Elsewhere, another curry soup recipe is based on 'a Knukle of Veal, an old fowl, or coarse piece of Beef'. The meat is boiled 'until all the strengths out of it', and a cup of rice added to the strained liquid. Further pieces of meat, dredged in curry powder and flour, were added after light browning in a frying pan.

Mulgatawy is made in the same way [as Gillsland curried chicken], but with less butter & mutton or veal stock instead of water & the fowl not cut but stewed till it falls in pieces. It is served in a Tureen.

The eastern theme is continued with the recipe for 'Indian pickle'. Here, cayenne pepper, ginger, mustard seed, white pepper, and cloves were added to white wine vinegar and salt brine to produce a preserving liquid. Stephana writes: 'you may then put in Melons, Cucumbers, Cauliflower, Horse-radish, Onions, Shallots, french beans, in short anything you please only let it be well dried before it is put in'.

Ketchups originated in China as dipping sauces. From China, they migrated to India via South-East Asia and reached Britain through samples brought back by the East India Company. At first, the name ketchup, or catsup as it was often known, was applied to what was really a mushroom sauce in which chopped, heavily salted and spiced mushrooms were boiled rapidly for short periods over several days. Elizabeth Cleland's instructions 'To make Ketchup' in her *New and Easy Method of Cookery* of 1755 is one such recipe. Stephana Malcolm's 'Mushroom Catsup' is similar.

[7] The word 'mulligatawny' comes from the Tamil 'milagu-tannir' meaning 'pepper water'.

Stephana has a 'White Catsup' much nearer to the original fish and brine pickle. In this recipe, a pound of anchovies are boiled in the best vinegar and then sieved prior to the addition of shallots, Madeira wine, and spices. A walnut ketchup was also made. All these sauces were based on a prepared spiced vinegar to which garlic, horseradish, or lemon-peel were added before boiling. As with the mushroom ketchup, the finished product was bottled, corked, and stored for future use.

Before these thinner sauces became popular it was usual to add spices directly to meat, fish, and vegetable dishes during cooking. As ketchups were meant to be long lasting, this became unnecessary. Hannah Glasse's recipe 'To make ketchup to keep twenty years' in her chapter aimed at sea-farers is an extreme example.[8] With such high expectations, ketchups were put away in the store cupboard and intended to last almost indefinitely, being brought out to season made-up dishes as required.

Although Stephana's diary is largely a record of social engagements, comments such as 'Today our cow was killed' and, the following day, 'Helped Andrew to cut up the cow', reveal that her life was not entirely pleasure-seeking. Meat continued to dominate the Scots diet, but as a proportion of the whole Stephana's recipe books include few made-up meat dishes, favouring sauces to pour over roasted or boiled flesh.

Stephana's sauces were freshly made for each dish, or, like the ketchups, prepared in quantity against future use. Sauces noted include 'liver sauce', 'sauce for a fillet of veal', 'sauce for roasted rabbits', 'white sauce for boiled fowls', and 'sauce for pork and beef stakes [steaks]'. Some of these sauces, like the rich 'sauce for a fillet of veal', are actually combinations of two different sauces, one prepared and one freshly made. This sauce consists of cream, sherry and 'a very small tea cup full of fish sauce', thickened with a roux of butter and flour.

Sauce for a Fillet of Veal

Mix 5 ozs of butter well with flour, melt it in half a pint of cream add to it a very small tea cup full of fish sauce and the same quantity of sherry the butter should be boiled after the fish sauce and wine are in.

Like so many of the prepared sauces, Stephana's 'fish sauce' was based on anchovies to which onions, spices, and herbs were added. The ingredients were then boiled for an hour in port wine and vinegar, strained, the spices removed, and then boiled again before being bottled and stored. Stephana's fish sauce was intended to add piquancy to what might otherwise be a bland dish.

The recipe books show very little interest in either fish or game. Apart from sauces for fish, the former are represented by 'To Collar Salmon', 'To spatchcock eels', and two kedgeree recipes. For game, there are sauces for rabbits and hares, a hare soup, and 'Rabbit with Onions'.

Recipes for vegetables are few and far between, and when they do occur are largely suggestions for preserving. Typical are the pickles based on garden vegetables such as mushrooms and onions. Mushrooms were a favourite subject for preservation, with mushroom pickles, ketchups, and mushroom powder all appearing. The latter involved placing the peeled mushrooms in a dripping pan, strew-

---

[8] Hannah Glasse, *The Art of Cookery, made Plain and Easy* (London, 1747), p. 121.

ing them with salt and leaving them to dry in an oven until brittle enough to beat to a powder. As with the sauces and ketchups, this was to be stored for future use: 'When it is fine, add to it a good quantity of Cayenne pepper, put it in a dry bottle, Cork it well and put it in a dry place'.

A few vegetable soups, notably artichoke, appear and there are wines such as 'Parsnip Wine'. Otherwise vegetables are under-represented, suggesting that they were either served as part of made-up meat or fish dishes or simply boiled. At Burnfoot, as in the Saltoun recipe books, at Ochtertyre, and in Mrs Cleland's cookery book, vegetable dishes are rare. Overall, vegetables were of little culinary interest to Stephana Malcolm. Potatoes, still something of a novelty, are the exception to the rule.

Stephana's 'Baked Potato Pudding' consists of potatoes, milk, brown sugar, nutmeg, and ginger, all fortified with half a glass of whisky. From Knockhill in Fife comes a non-alcoholic version, this time made with eggs. For 'Potato Crusted Pie', mashed potatoes were placed over sliced cold meat covered with well-seasoned gravy. A later addition to Stephana's recipe books is a recipe, dated 1809, for a 'Luncheon Dish' from Carberry Tower in East Lothian. This is a cheap, convenient dish for using left-over pieces of cold roast beef or mutton. The seasoned, finely-minced meat was mixed with gravy before being encased in mashed potato and browned before the fire. Potato puffs are a fried version of the same.

POTATO PUFFS

Take cold meat clear it from the gristle mince it & sesson it with salt pepper & a small quantity of pickles cut small, boil and mash some Potatoes make them into a paste with one or two Eggs, roll it out with a dust of flour, cut it round with a saucer, put some of your seasoned meat in one half, fold the other over it like a puff, nick it neatly round, & fry it light brown.

Stephana Malcolm was of a solid and respected if somewhat impecunious family. Her cookery books are practical but at the same time reflect those aspects of diet thought suitable concerns for a young lady. Recipes for preserving fruit and vegetables from the kitchen garden and orchard are important, as are dainty cakes and tea-breads to put before her numerous guests at the 'four hours'. Stephana had the leisure to experiment with new fruits, such as rhubarb, and new dishes, both those gleaned from her English relatives and brought home from the East by her brothers. In spite of its cosmopolitan outlook, however, compared with George Dalrymple's *The Practice of Modern Cookery*, published in Edinburgh in 1781, Stephana's recipes appear homely.

Dalrymple's cookery book was dedicated to Lady Whitefoord, the wife of his former employer, Sir John Whitefoord, 'as a small mark of respect for her Ladyship's judgement'. While exploiting his aristocratic links, the subtitle of Dalrymple's book shows that his intended market was Scotland's expanding well-to-do middle classes. His recipes were, 'Adapted to Families of Distinction as well as those of the Middling Ranks of Life'. Dalrymple's book is comprehensive and he freely admits that not all of the recipes are original: 'I do not pretend all the merit myself. There are a number of excellent receipts I have had occasionally from others, which it would have been a pity to have withheld'.

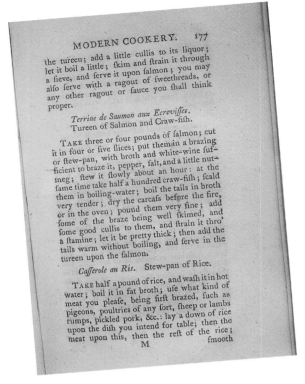

George Dalrymple, The Practice of Modern Cookery *(Edinburgh, 1781).*

George Dalrymple was a professional chef, at one time in the employ of Sir John Whitefoord. As an exponent of 'haute cuisine', Dalrymple's intended market was the expanding ranks of Scotland's middle-classes.

National Library of Scotland.

Dalrymple was an exponent of 'haute cuisine'. This is special-occasion cooking with recipes such as 'Small chickens with preserved Nectarines', and 'Legs of Fowls Bacchus-fashion'. Many, in the late eighteenth century, must have aspired to such extravagant, high-class cookery, and herein lies much of the book's appeal. However, cookery of this nature was not to everyone's taste, and had it been known to Thomas Hudleston, author of a *New Method of Cookery*, published in Dumfries in 1760, the book would surely have qualified as one of those he dismissed as 'stuff'd with superfluous trifles'.

At the other end of the social scale, *The Statistical Account of Scotland*, compiled by parish ministers in the 1790s, gives an indication of the diet of the ordinary Scot.[9] Then, a typical farmer's family from a Perthshire parish existed on oatmeal, barley-meal, potatoes, and cheese. While many kept a few cattle, a large proportion of these animals were exported on the hoof in droves as a cash-crop. As a result, a family might have just one salted bullock to last them the entire winter. This, together with a sheep in the spring and joints of mutton purchased occasionally throughout the year, as funds permitted, was all the meat they could expect. Such a diet, heavily reliant on oatmeal, was rich in starch and protein but undoubtedly mineral deficient. Milk, and kail in the soup, helped remedy this to some extent.

In the midst of all their plenty it is easy to lose sight of just how far removed both Stephana Malcolm and George Dalrymple's cuisine was from that of the

[9] *The Statistical Account of Scotland, 1791-1799: North and West Perthshire*, ed. by Donald J. Withrington and Ian R. Grant (1977), XII.

Interior of a Highland cottage, Katharine Jane Ellice, c.1860.
The lifestyle of Stephana Malcolm and George Dalrymple bore little resemblance to that of the majority of Scots. *National Library of Scotland, MS.15174, no.2.*

ordinary folk of Scotland. Dalrymple's cookery book was intended for people to aspire to, not for daily use as a working tool. The remarkable series of recipe books of the Malcolm of Burnfoot family, covering four generations and over a hundred years of culinary history, consists of dishes which could be created in most reasonably wealthy households. With their cosmopolitan outlook, and emphasis firmly on the novel (both in new ingredients and cooking methods), they are much more representative of actual innovations in eating habits in Scotland at the turn of the eighteenth century.

THE

COOK AND HOUSEWIFE'S
MANUAL;

CONTAINING THE

MOST APPROVED MODERN RECEIPTS

FOR MAKING

SOUPS, GRAVIES, SAUCES, RAGOUTS, AND
MADE-DISHES;

AND FOR PIES, PUDDINGS, PASTRY, PICKLES,
AND PRESERVES;

ALSO

FOR BAKING, BREWING, MAKING HOME-MADE
WINES, CORDIALS, &c.

THE WHOLE

ILLUSTRATED BY NUMEROUS NOTES, AND PRACTICAL
OBSERVATIONS, ON ALL THE VARIOUS BRANCHES
OF DOMESTIC ECONOMY.

BY MRS MARGARET DODS,
OF THE CLEIKUM INN, ST RONAN'S.

"'Be sharp and prompt in' Cook, see all your cover-
Be sharp and prompt in the palate, that they may
Commend you; look to your meat and boiled meats handsomely,
And what new kitchens and entrants made things."

Beaumont and Fletcher.

EDINBURGH;
PRINTED FOR THE AUTHOR,
AND SOLD BY BELL & BRADFUTE,
EDINBURGH; LONGMAN, REES, ORME, BROWN, AND
GREEN, LONDON; ROBERTSON, AND ATKINSON,
GLASGOW; AND JOHN CUMMING, DUBLIN.

1826.

7 TURKEY FIGS, AMERICAN APPLES AND DUTCH CHEESE

BOWLAND, 1836-1860

'Kitchen and Scullery - 3 tables 1 leg loose, 6(5) chairs, meal chest, fixed pestle and mortar, Grate and key for ditto, Fender, Poker Tongs and Shovel (Shovel Old).'

AS WAS THE CUSTOM OF MANY NEW WIVES, SHORTLY AFTER HER MARRIAGE ELIZA WALKER took an inventory of the contents of her new home.[1] In doing so, she had no need to start a new volume as one was already in existence: Eliza's mother-in-law, Barbara Walker, began the inventory in 1811 when she listed the linen at Bowland House. Over the years, the inventory was updated several times (by Eliza in 1836, and finally in 1852) to provide a comprehensive listing of the entire furnishings of the house from attic to cellar.

Bowland House, 1907. Royal Commission on the Ancient and Historical Monuments of Scotland. By permission of Charles Hind.

In 1836, the small estate of Bowland near Galashiels in the Scottish Borders had not long been in the possession of the Walker family. The property was bought in 1810 by Brigadier-General Alexander Walker on his retirement after twenty years of military and administrative service in India.

Purchase of the estate in Selkirkshire was soon followed by marriage to Barbara Montgomery. The Walkers divided their time between Edinburgh and Bowland, where the Brigadier involved himself in agricultural improvement. In 1822 he was tempted out of retirement to govern St Helena, accompanied by his wife and two young sons. In spite of his age, Walker was an active administrator. While there, he was involved in agricultural improvement, founded schools and libraries, established farming and gardening societies and even introduced the natives

[1] National Library of Scotland, Walker of Bowland papers, MS.14051.

to silkworm culture. Walker returned to Bowland with his family in 1828. Unfortunately, both he and his wife died shortly afterwards, in 1831.

Alexander Walker's son, William Stuart Walker, studied at Oxford before entering the legal profession, being admitted Advocate in 1840. In 1836, he married Eliza Loch, daughter of George Loch of the Bengal Civil Service. A prominent member of the Scottish Episcopal Church, Walker was appointed Secretary to the Board of Supervision in 1852, a position he occupied until 1892.

William Walker's work as an advocate meant that he had to spend much of his time in Edinburgh while his family remained at Bowland. At first he lived in a property in George Square on the south side of Edinburgh, not far from Argyle Square, where James and Margaret Erskine had lived in the 1750s (see Chapter 5).

William Walker was much missed by his wife, and Eliza wrote to him regularly, often on a daily basis.[2] In January 1840 she wrote, 'My dearest husband, It really is melancholy that I am again reduced to have recourse to Pen and ink, as my only means of having a little loving conversation with you'. Preoccupied with domestic detail, Eliza's letters provide a wealth of information of the minutiae of daily life in this comfortable family home.

There is much in the letters of the eating and drinking habits of the family. So, Eliza reminds her husband 'Please don't forget to order the Sherry – we have commenced the last bottle'. She even recounts the occasion on which the housekeeper forgot to serve the toast. Game shot by members of the family reached the table. Eliza writes: 'I send you by tomorrow morning's coach six Rabbits – which will come in handy sans doute . . . I have sent the hare to Windydoors. We had an excellent one at dinner today – one of those you shot a fortnight ago'. Later, Eliza writes of the 'beautiful pheasant which formed . . . my repast this evening. It was the cock pheasant you shot when you first came out here, and really a splendid looking bird'.

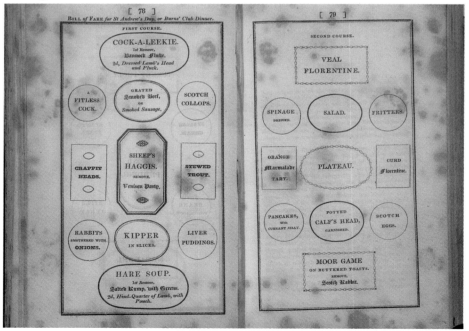

Table-settings for 'A Dinner of Seven Dishes' and a 'St Andrews Day or Burns' Club Dinner' from Margaret Dods, The Cook and Housewife's Manual (Edinburgh, 1826).
The first courses suggested here by Meg Dods differ little from those served at Saltoun a century earlier. However, the second courses are much lighter, with greater prominence given to desserts. National Library of Scotland.

[2] National Library of Scotland, Walker of Bowland papers, MSS.13962-3.

The dining room at Castle Fraser.
National Trust for Scotland.

Dinner parties were a feature of William Walker's life in Edinburgh. Like many an anxious wife, Eliza was concerned that he should not overindulge: 'You are prudence itself, and I bestow on you the highest approbation for taking such care, and resisting such various delicate temptations in the shape of Mr Fletcher's sundry eatables and drinkables displayed at his hospitable board'. She went on to regret that Mr Fletcher 'has never given me his promised receipt for the oyster omelet'.

Bills of Fare, depicting both ideal and real meals (like those of a century earlier in the Fletcher of Saltoun papers – see page 41), give some indication as to what was customarily set on the dinner-tables of the wealthy. Meg Dods's *The Cook and Housewife's Manual* of 1826 includes a number of such diagrams and provides an indication of the differences and similarities in dining habits in the 1720s and the 1820s. Meg Dods's menu for a 'Dinner of Seven Dishes' is typical of her time. As in the Saltoun menu of the 1720s, there was skate with anchovy and butter. This was replaced by a remove of a joint of lamb with mint sauce. The rest of the first course, consisting of Lobster Patties, brown soup, stewed rump and greens, Oxford Dumplings, carrots and broccoli was much the same as that served at Saltoun, save that greater emphasis was placed on the vegetable dishes.

The second courses, however, were very different. In the Saltoun menu this was a lighter course, consisting of shell-fish, poultry, and vegetables. Although the poultry and vegetables remained, desserts were more important in Meg Dods's menu of a century later. In this example, both an almond pudding and Italian Cream were served.

The appearance of Meg Dods's *The Cook and Housewife's Manual* in 1826 is of some significance in the history of Scottish cookery. Margaret Dods was the landlady of the inn in Sir Walter Scott's novel *St Ronan's Well*. The author of the cookery book was actually Isobel Christian Johnston. Married to an Edinburgh publisher, she was well-known in Edinburgh literary circles as the author of several works of fiction and editor of *Tait's Magazine*. Mrs Johnston is also known as a friend of Sir Walter Scott. Although Scott's role in the cookery book is un-certain, there is little doubt that he wrote the introduction.[3]

The lengthy introduction to Meg Dods's cookery book served to explain the motive for writing the book. 'Scotland has absolutely retrograded in gastronomy; yet she saw a better day', bemoans Peregrine Touchwood, one of Scott's characters from *St Ronan's Well*. Touchwood, and his English companion, 'the celebrated churchman and gourmand' Dr Redgill, deep in their cups, enlist the assistance of their landlady, Meg Dods, a notable cook, to set matters aright. This they do by instituting the Cleikum Club at the meetings of which lectures on cookery are to be given for the benefit of the nation's cuisine.

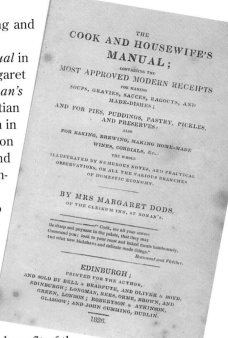

Margaret Dods, The Cook and Housewife's Manual *(Edinburgh, 1826).*
The author of this cookery book was actually Isobel Johnston, a respected figure in Edinburgh literary circles. Margaret Dods was the landlady in Sir Walter Scott's novel *St Ronan's Well*.
National Library of Scotland.

Mrs Johnston (alias Meg Dods) is not alone in lamenting the decline in the standard of cookery in the early nineteenth century. Rather, this is a recurring theme in recipe books of the time. In his *Cook's Oracle*, the English cookery writer Dr Kitchiner is particularly vehement in his condemnation of the lack of skill among contemporary cooks.

Isobel Johnston's cookery book was aimed at the mistresses of the growing numbers of middle-class families. Written in a light-hearted and yet informative way, her work was well received on publication. There is much useful information about the availability of produce as well as helpful advice on selecting foodstuffs, cookery, and presentation. For the modern cook, her chief defect is her failure to provide precise information about quantities, cooking times and temperatures, something which we have come to expect today.

Meg Dods includes a chapter on Scottish national dishes. Starting with 'The Scotch Haggis', there are recipes for cock-a-leekie soup, hotch-potch, crappit heads[4] and sheep's head broth. She also attested to the continued importance of broth in the Scottish diet in 1826 when she claimed it as 'the only true foundation to the principal repast of the day'. She adds: 'the French take the lead of all European people in soups and broths . . . the SCOTCH rank second, the Welsh next, and the English . . . are at the very bottom of the scale'.[5] Otherwise, many recipes and cooking methods are similar to those in Eliza Acton's *Modern Cookery for Private*

---

[3] Although Scott did not acknowledge writing the introduction, *The Monthly Review* noted that if it were not by Scott himself, the author 'has presented us with an imitation of the great novelist . . . remarkable for its fidelity, facility and cleverness'.

[4] A forcemeat consisting originally of oatmeal, suet, onions, and seasonings. Later, lobster or crab meat, anchovy, eggs, oyster sauce, and cayenne pepper were added.

[5] Dods, p. 64.

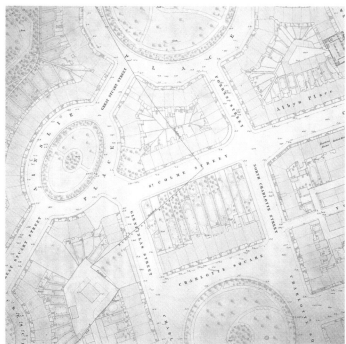

St Colme Street, Edinburgh. Detail from the Ordnance Survey series 'Edinburgh and its Environs', 1:1056, published 1852-1855. National Library of Scotland.

Families, first published in London in 1845. Once again, this is indicative of the trend towards a common British cuisine.

By 1843, the Walkers had purchased a larger townhouse, 7 St Colme Street, in the New Town of Edinburgh. There, the family's neighbours included several other members of the legal profession, notably the Lord Advocate. The street was favoured by the gentry, the former occupant of number seven being Sir Kenneth Mackenzie of Coul. At the other end of the street lived the Misses Cadell of Tranent, relatives of the Cadells of Grange. It was to St Colme Street, in the heart of fashionable Edinburgh, that Eliza and the children came to join William in 1846. Not having the same need to write to each other, few letters between William and Eliza survive after this date.

Bowland House remained the family's main residence, and it is this property to which the household inventory relates. The furnishings of the dining room at Bowland indicate the elegance and comfort of the homes of the wealthy in the mid-nineteenth century. Pride of place went to the four mahogany dining tables, the twelve mahogany chairs, and the matching mahogany sideboard. On this sideboard sat the three mahogany knife and spoon cases. The dumb waiter, plate warmer, table brush, and brass-handled toasting fork completed the room. Twenty pictures on the walls of the room looked down on the scene.

The furnishings of the dining room were far from new. The curtains were soiled, and there was a large stain in the carpet. The chairs, too, had seen better days, with '15 small Nobs awanting 1 leg broken and 2 splades damaged and 1 top rail and several frames loose'. Finally, in an endearingly human touch, the note of the patent corkscrew is accompanied by the comment – 'useless'.

A separate page in the inventory is reserved for the 'Dining Room Press' containing most of the family crystal. Finger glasses are followed by wine coolers,

The china cupboard at the Georgian House, Edinburgh. National Trust for Scotland.

large and small ale glasses, green hock glasses, champagne glasses, liqueur glasses, plain, globe and cut wine glasses. After the glasses come the wine and claret decanters, cruet bottles and earthenware wine coolers. With comments such as 'two patterns', 'cracked' and 'slightly chipped', it is easy to imagine Eliza painstakingly listing the contents of her house.

While the best china was kept in the 'Dining Room Press', other less valuable crockery was distributed throughout the house. Much of the family's china was stored under the watchful eye of the housekeeper. The 'china closet' in her room was home to a complete dinner service with tureens, stands and covers, corner dishes and covers, salad bowls, a fish drainer, soup plates, and various sizes of matching plates. In addition, there were breakfast and china sets, muffin dishes and covers, milk jugs, bread plates, cream jugs, and cups and saucers, not to mention glass dishes for honey, butter, and preserves, with their matching covers and stands. The green breakfast china was kept in the Butler's Pantry with the common dessert set.

The butler's duties in the mid-nineteenth century were much the same as those of the Ochtertyre butler in 1763. He still supervised the work of the male servants, and had important duties with regard to food and drink for the family. The contents of the cellar were his responsibility, as were the cleaning and polishing of the household's silver and cutlery. He was also expected to pay all the bills not paid by the housekeeper, to answer the door, and to care for his master's clothes where no valet was employed.

The Butler's Pantry at Bowland housed a variety of items appropriate to his role: there were tea trays, carving knives of various sizes, nut crackers, japanned night lights and corkscrews. Even a broken beer cork, cheese stand, 'key for door', candles, and glass lantern are listed.

The kitchen and scullery together occupy over five pages of the inventory. This was more than for any other room in the house, as at Ochtertyre. The inventory opens with the cooking equipment. High on the list come two ovens and a Dutch oven, and two large boilers. There was a stand for heating irons, a hot plate, grate, fender, a smoke jack,[6] tongs, poker, and a meat screen.[7]

The kitchen at the Georgian House, Edinburgh. National Trust for Scotland.

[6] Smoke jacks, used to power revolving roasting spits, came to Britain in the second half of the eighteenth century. The fan of the jack was fixed in the chimney. Hot air from the fire caused it to revolve and so turned the spit.

[7] A heat-reflecting metal screen suspended over the fire which speeded up the cooking process.

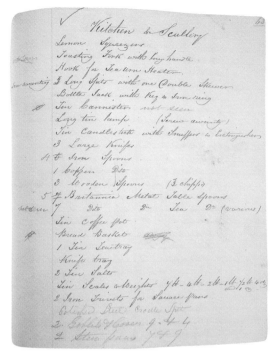

Inventory of the contents of the kitchen at Bowland House taken by Eliza Walker in 1836. The pencil annotations were made in 1852. National Library of Scotland, MS.14051, f.63.

Given the equipment in the kitchen, at least some of the cooking at Bowland must have used the open fire as a source of heat, with the food being placed in suspended cauldrons, or actually placed among the embers in utensils such as the Dutch oven. The two ovens of the inventory were probably set into the wall at the side of the fire.

The earliest enclosed kitchen range was designed by Thomas Robinson in 1780.[8] His range had an open coal fire with metal hobs on either side. At one side there was a built-in iron oven with a hinged door, and on the other an iron tank for hot water. Although this was a considerable advance, the food in the oven tended to cook unevenly, as the heat came from one side only. Later, the open fire in the centre was enclosed with a metal hotplate on which pans could be placed. Several designs of enclosed ranges became available in the early nineteenth century, one of the best-known being Count Rumford's.

The kitchen at Bowland housed an impressive *batterie de cuisine*. Listed are a coffee mill, a pepper mill, and a 'box with vegetable cutter'. Among the pans are large stock pots, frying pans, metal fish kettles, stew pans, gridirons, a dripping pan, a Yorkshire Pudding pan, and open tart pans. Additional items include a cake toaster, a griddle, brass preserving pans, copper warming pans, copper moulds, a cutlet pan, casserole moulds, cream moulds, a bread basket, wooden spoons, iron trivets, and lemon squeezers.

The Walkers must have employed several live-in servants. As well as the Housekeeper's Room and the Butler's Pantry, there was a 'Maid Servants' Room' with two beds and four mattresses and a 'Man Servants' Room' containing six beds. Dining facilities were provided in the Servants' Hall.

While the households of the aristocracy had been extensive for centuries, in Victorian Britain the trend to employ servants spread to the middle classes. The result was that the married woman was increasingly not expected to do any domestic work. She discussed menus and the daily routine of the household with her housekeeper, but a small army of servants actually did the work. The middle-class housewife joined her wealthier sisters in a seemingly endless round of visits to friends, the sick, and the poor. When she chose to stay at home, her days would be occupied in reading, sewing, or drawing. Judging by her correspondence, Eliza Walker occupied much of her time in writing lengthy letters.

Just as Mrs Dudgeon had kept house for Lord and Lady Alva in the 1750s, so now Mr and Mrs Walker could afford to employ a housekeeper. If Mrs Dudgeon had a wide choice of shops available to her in Edinburgh from which to purchase household goods, then Eliza Walker and her housekeeper had a much greater wealth of small shops to choose from a century later. For the food trades alone the Edinburgh Post Office Directories include entries for bakers, cheesemongers, confectioners, fishmongers, fleshers (butchers), fruiterers, grocers, poulterers,

[8] Yarwood, pp. 84-90.

Detail from Joseph Ebsworth, 'North View of Edinburgh from the Upper Gallery of the Scott Monument', showing bustling Princes Street shops, 1847. National Library of Scotland.

tea dealers, and vintners. Galashiels, too, had its share of small businesses in the retail food trade.

The Walker family patronised several tradesmen, remaining loyal to favoured shopkeepers for more than twenty years. Their accounts with tradesmen in Edinburgh and Galashiels are entered in no fewer than seventy-six volumes dating from 1830 to 1860.[9] This extensive series of account books provides a detailed record of one family's daily spending on food and gives some indication of their eating habits over thirty years.

The notebooks are typically headed, 'Mr Walker, 7 St Colme Street, in account with Andrew Melrose, Grocer, 93 George Street'. Although the writer is not identified, the housekeeper, and not the lady of the house, dealt with most of the tradesmen on a daily basis. The small volume entitled simply 'Cook's Book' notes purchases of eggs, oatmeal, sugar, herrings,and barley as well as black lead for the kitchen range. These were small-scale purchases and were probably made from street traders or hawkers at the back door of the house.

Between 1839 and 1846 the Walker family purchased meat from James Smart, an Edinburgh flesher. During the winter months, meat was usually bought every fourth day. In the days before refrigeration, even this was too long an interval in the summer-time, when meat was often bought in daily. Vast quantities were purchased: in 1845, the annual meat bill was over £135. In February 1845 no less than 258 lb of beef and mutton, 7 lb of veal, 4 lb of tripe, and four sheep's heads were bought. Later in the same year, in May 1845, purchases were almost on the same scale. Then, the family consumed 220 lb of beef and mutton, three quarters of lamb, 3 lb of tripe and four sheep's heads.

[9] National Library of Scotland, Walker of Bowland papers, MSS.13968-4044.

Tradesmen's account books kept by the Walker of Bowland family, 1854-1863.
National Library of Scotland, MSS. 14016, 14020, 14044.

As the numbers living and eating in the Erskine and Walker households at any given time are not known, it is impossible to make precise comparisons of their relative consumption of meat. However, the quantities involved for both households are large. By the early nineteenth century, agricultural improvements, notably in selective breeding and the provision of foodstuffs for animals, had led to a great improvement in the condition of Scottish cattle. As a result, there was now a steady supply of butcher meat available. Clearly, meat was of great importance in the diet of the Walker family.

As in the Erskine household almost a century earlier, beef and mutton were purchased regularly, and beef in greater quantities than mutton. Both in Edinburgh and when at Bowland, the Walker family usually ate fresh meat. With a ready supply of butcher meat available, the need to eat salt or pickled beef was removed. Only on a few occasions during the winter months was any salted beef bought.

Often the accounts simply refer to the quantity of meat purchased, but sometimes specific joints or cuts of beef such as sirloin, steak, rump, shoulder, and hough are mentioned. Most parts of the animal were considered edible, and tripe, tongue, ox feet, ox bladders, ox heart, spare ribs, sweetbreads, and marrow bones were all bought.

Veal was popular. The reason for this is probably that, in spite of the recent advances in agricultural methods, the breeding of beef cattle was still in its infancy. Coming from such young animals, cuts of veal were almost certain to be tender. Purchases of up to 5 lb of veal were made as often as two or three times a month. Now and then, a calf's head appeared on the table. Veal cutlets and fillets were a particular favourite in St Colme Street. They may well have been prepared according to the instructions for simple breaded veal cutlets given by Cecilia Combe, wife of the renowned Scottish phrenologist, George Combe.[10]

VEAL CUTLETS

Take the ribs of small veal & when separated & [made] tender with a broad knife, place them in a mixture of fine breadcrumbs nutmeg salt, and chopped parsley - turn them often - melt butter and clarify it - put the chops with the clarified butter on the fire, put into a covered pan & let them cook half an hour.

Mutton appears more often in the accounts than veal. Joints of mutton, sheep's head, mutton chops, and gigot of mutton are all mentioned. The French word 'gigot', meaning leg of lamb or mutton, was still quite new to Scots cooks: its first use in a Scots cookery book was in Mrs Maciver's *Cookery and Pastry-making* of 1773. By this time the term was also in use in English recipe books.[11] Both Scots and English cooks probably borrowed the word from the French. Lamb is mentioned only from time to time, as it was used to describe only very young animals.

When in Edinburgh, the Walkers bought their fish from a specialist fishmonger, John Jameson of 79 Queen Street. Fish was clearly popular, as purchases were made several times a week throughout the year, and sometimes daily. A wide

[10] National Library of Scotland, Combe papers, MS.7468, f.8v. The notebook is undated, but is probably of the 1840s.

[11] Hope, *A Caledonian Feast*, p. 295.

variety of fish and shell-fish was available, of which the Walkers took full advantage. On 5 November 1847 they bought lobster, brill, fifty oysters and a crab. Also for sale were salmon, whiting, herring, haddock, crab, trout, sparling, sole, findon (haddock),[12] flounders, halibut, cod, and shrimps.

A SAVOURY SHRIMP OR PRAWN PIE MAIGRE
Have as many well cleaned shrimps or prawns as will nearly fill the pie-dish. Season with pounded mace, cloves, a little Cayenne and Chili vinegar. Put some butter in the dish, and cover with a light puff paste. Less than three quarters of an hour will bake them.[13]

Between 1840 and 1842 bread was bought from Alexander Learmonth, a general retailer who also sold dairy products and potatoes. Later, the Walkers patronised a specialist baker, William Gray. While the bread bought from Learmonth is not specified, it probably differed from that baked by Gray. The latter had a range of baked goods for sale, and there are purchases of 'half a brown loaf' at three pence half-penny; 'loaves fine' cost nine pence, and ordinary loaves sixpence each. Bread was bought at least once every three days. Later, Thomas Weir supplied the household with a variety of loaves, rolls, and the increasingly popular sweetened breads.

Fruit came from Daniel Ferguson, a specialist fruiterer. His accounts indicate the seasonal nature of the trade. In the summer, pints of strawberries, raspberries, cherries, and gooseberries were bought. Apricots, pears, greengage plums, grapes, damsons, and a variety of apples were in the shop in the autumn. Baking, table, and roasting apples are noted separately, as are 'Ribston apples'. In November there were Jordan almonds at one shilling and sixpence per pound and green walnuts, raisins, and dates. December saw the appearance of chestnuts and prunes, together with dried apples, figs, and oranges. In January and February virtually the only fruit bought was oranges, entered either simply as oranges or 'marmalade oranges'. More imported fruit was for sale in March when the family bought French prunes, Turkey figs, and American apples, twenty-four of which cost two shillings and sixpence. Some imported fruits, notably lemons, were available all year round. Others, such as the Turkey figs and apples from America, were bought in to stock the shelves at times when home-grown produce was in short supply.

Daniel Ferguson did not sell vegetables. The family bought these from another specialist, Miss E. Tran, a greengrocer with a shop in Queen Street, Edinburgh. As perishable goods, vegetables were purchased almost daily. Invariably, the order starts with a peck of potatoes at three pence. The quantities involved suggest that they were now part of the daily fare. Meg Dods writes that 'potatoes are of the most consequence'. She goes on to instruct on how to 'boil, roast . . . ragout, fry and mash' them. As with fruit, purchases of vegetables were, of necessity, seasonal. Cauliflower, sprouts, turnips, carrots, celery, savoys, spinach, and

Account book of the Walkers of Bowland with Daniel Ferguson, Fruiterer, Edinburgh, 1846.
National Library of Scotland, MS.13984, f.3v.

[12] The villagers of Findon, a few miles south of Aberdeen, have produced a distinctive smoked haddock, dried over the smoke of seaweed, since at least the eighteenth century.

[13] Dods, p. 127.

'Fisherfolk', Katharine Jane Ellice, c.1850. National Library of Scotland, MS.15173, no.28.

onions were bought in winter. In the summer months came peas, broccoli, asparagus, beetroot, cabbage, and cucumbers.

Meg Dods tells of recent improvements in the quality of vegetables and the quantity grown. Twenty years previously, she wrote, only turnips, carrots, and leeks were found on gentlemen's tables and then as luxury items. The evidence of numerous family records, including those of Saltoun, and of John Reid's *The Scots Gard'ner*, suggest that she was mistaken. What seems more likely is that the range of vegetables known to the very wealthy for centuries was now more widely available.

Meg Dods's instructions for cooking vegetables are aimed at those new to this branch of cookery. There are directions for preparing vegetables, and proper methods of cleaning. On cooking, 'All vegetables should be enough boiled. The cook's rule of having them *crisp*, is as inimical to health as offensive to the palate'.

Of more relevance to the modern cook are the suggestions for vegetable dishes such as artichokes in a rich white or brown sauce, broccoli on toast, turnips with powdered ginger, roasted onions, and stewed cucumbers.

Miss Tran, the greengrocer, did not confine herself to vegetables. She also sold a wide range of fruit. The Walkers bought rhubarb, gooseberries, apples, cherries, and strawberries from her. Herbs, notably mint and parsley, also came from Miss Tran's shop, as did dairy products such as cream and sweet milk, imported lemons and figs, and sundries, including salt and sand.

'Vegetable and Fish Market, from the "Rainbow" Gallery', in Thomas Shepherd, Modern Athens, Displayed in a Series of Views, or Edinburgh in the Nineteenth Century (London, 1828). National Library of Scotland.

Dried goods came from the grocer. From 1846 to 1853 William Walker had an account with an Edinburgh grocer, Andrew Melrose. Melrose's entry in the Edinburgh Post Office Directory for 1847-1848 describes his company as 'Tea-dealers to the Queen and Grocers', suggesting that this was a high-class business. At the time he operated from two prime sites in central Edinburgh: 93 George Street and 122 High Street. An earlier Directory, for 1840-1841, lists another shop in nearby South Bridge.

Selling dried goods such as sugar, rice, tapioca, semolina, tea, and coffee, together with imported and prepared foodstuffs, household goods such as soap, black lead, and starch, the grocer's shop provided both everyday and luxury goods

and played an important role in the domestic economy. This is reflected in the high proportion of grocers' shops to the total number of retail outlets in most British towns and cities.[14]

Sugar was available from the grocer in a variety of forms. Raw sugar was the cheapest, at five pence per pound; candied sugar, at one shilling per pound, was the most expensive. In between came pounded (ground), loaf, grated, and crushed sugar. To produce loaf sugar, liquid sugar was poured into conical moulds varying in size between one and three feet high. Once in the home, the required amount of sugar was cut off using sugar cutters, the loaf being held in place by special grippers. Sugar appears in quantities of up to 10 lb several times on most pages of the Walker family's accounts, and its importance in the diet is clear.

Shortbread has been made in Scotland for centuries. In 1608, the Earl of Angus bought shortbread from a Glasgow baker. Towards the end of the seventeenth century Lady Grisell Baillie gave instructions to her housekeeper for a 'short bread' made from a flour and butter mixture to which a little sugar was added. By the nineteenth century the proportions had changed with sugar becoming a major ingredient.

SHORT BREAD

To half a peck of flour, put a pound & half of butter, half a pound of Sugar, half a pound of Carraways, a quarter pound of Almonds & the same of Orange-peel – Mix all these together and bake them in the oven.
Mrs Lindsay of Eaglescarnie

This recipe for shortbread is taken from Margaret Stewart's recipe book.[15] Margaret was the wife of the Reverend Andrew Stewart, Minister of Erskine, who was a medical doctor as well as a clergyman. His medical training was used to good effect when he successfully treated his wife for pulmonary disease. Margaret Stewart began her recipe book in 1799 and continued to make entries up to 1839. Her shortbread recipe, given to her by Mrs Lindsay of Eaglescarnie, includes a good deal of sugar together with almonds (presumably ground), orange-peel and carraway seeds.

The dry goods bought from Andrew Melrose's shop by the Walker family include a high proportion of commercially prepared items. Marketed convenience foods became important in the late eighteenth century, and must have been a boon for the busy cook. Bottled sauces were among the first such foods. Used as condiments to season made dishes, they were prepared in large quantities from seasonal gluts of fruit and vegetables. Preserved in vinegar, brine or spices, like their home-made equivalents, these sauces would keep for months or even for years. For this reason, they did not represent the same risk to the retailer as more perishable goods.

On 8 May 1848, Mrs Walker bought bottles of lemon essence, vanilla essence, lemon pickle, 'Harveys sauce'[16] and tomato pickle from Andrew Melrose. Toma-

'Short Bread', from Margaret Stewart's recipe book, 1799-1835. Shortbread has been made in Scotland for centuries. In the seventeenth century, it consisted of a butter and flour mixture. By Margaret Stewart's time, sugar had become a major ingredient. National Library of Scotland, MS.24777, f.8.

[14] Dorothy Davis, *A History of Shopping* (London, 1966).

[15] National Library of Scotland, MS.24777.

[16] Lemon pickle was made by softening the fruit in spiced vinegar and passing it through a hair-sieve. Harveys sauce was made to a recipe devised by an English innkeeper, Peter Harvey, in the eighteenth century. It was widely marketed and gained considerable popularity.

toes had first been encountered by Westerners when the Spanish reached Mexico in 1519. The 'orange-yellow' tomato they brought back with them was known variously as the 'golden apple' or 'love-apple', and was thought to be an aphrodisiac. Although it was quickly incorporated into the Spanish, and somewhat later, the Italian diet, the tomato was regarded with considerable suspicion in Britain. It was not until the mid-eighteenth century that tomatoes began to appear in British recipe books. Most early British tomato recipes are for pickles and sauces.[17]

While the Walkers bought single jars of pickles and essences, 'Dutch cheese' and 'Gouda cheese' were purchased in large quantities. On 29 December 1848 they bought ten-and-a-half pounds, and another eleven-and-a-half pounds on 3 February 1849. Sometimes, there is an entry simply for 'cheese'. It is possible that this referred to a locally produced cheese, perhaps from one of the specialist cheesemongers in Edinburgh. Certainly, the cook's account books show that she took it on herself to buy 'cheas' from time to time.[18] Nonetheless, the accounts of purchases from Andrew Melrose's shop show that the family had undeniably developed a taste for cheese imported from the Netherlands.

Coffee, sometimes described as 'mocha coffee', is mentioned now and then. Usually, it was bought about once a month by the half pound for the then sizeable sum of £1 1s. Black tea (bohea) at five shillings per pound was considerably cheaper. The Walker family consumed up to 3 lb of tea a month. While tea remained popular with the wealthy, it had now reached down to the poorest members of society and was fast replacing ale as the staple drink.

This trend is confirmed by the sales ledger of an unidentified Edinburgh grocer for 1819 to 1834.[19] One of his customers, George Watson, a Bonnyrigg weaver, bought small quantities of tea several times a week, usually paying no more than ten pence a time. Another, Lady Seaforth, paid twelve shillings for her 2 lb of tea in January 1825. She bought no more until May when she purchased another 2 lb. To a large extent, tea had lost its luxury status and had become a necessity. Coffee remained a drink for the affluent for years to come.

Turkey figs, American apples, and Dutch cheese, bought from the grocer, were all eaten regularly in the Walker household. Luxury items such as these were not available to the general population, not least because the high cost of transport put them beyond the reach of the vast majority. Although commodities such as tea and sugar were affordable for many of the ordinary people, overall the Scottish diet was still very much limited to what could be produced locally, and by seasonal factors: harvest failure inevitably meant that the poor went hungry.

While poverty was still the lot of the masses, as the nineteenth century progressed the differences between the cookery of wealthy Scots and English lessened. Even in 1826, the recipes in Meg Dods's *The Cook and Housewife's Manual* bear some resemblance to those in Eliza Acton's *Modern Cookery* of 1845. Since a considerable number of the Scottish aristocracy and gentry were educated, worked, and spent much of their leisure time south of the Border, this is hardly surprising. Together with developments in transport, notably the appearance of the railways, better roads and steam ships, and improved techniques of food preservation, the trend towards a national British cuisine was to accelerate.

[17] Alexander Hunter, *Culina famulatrix medicinae, or receipts on modern cookery* (York, 1804).

[18] National Library of Scotland, Walker of Bowland papers, MS.13982, f.1v.

[19] National Library of Scotland, Acc.6074.

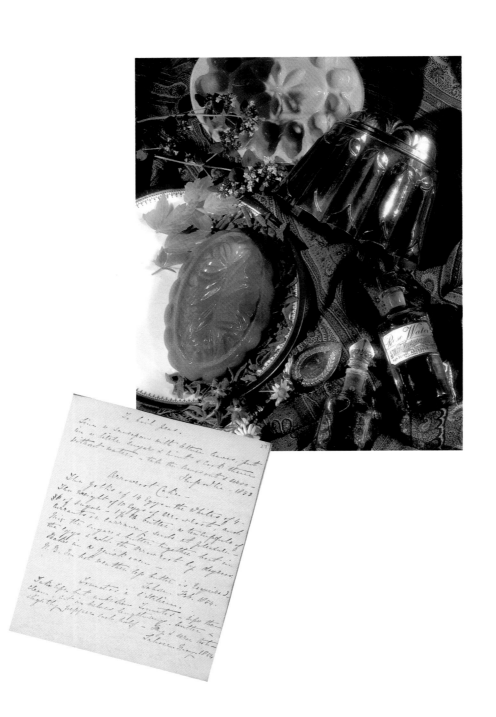

8 CHOCOLATE, TOMATOES AND CRAPPIT HEIDS

1847-1910

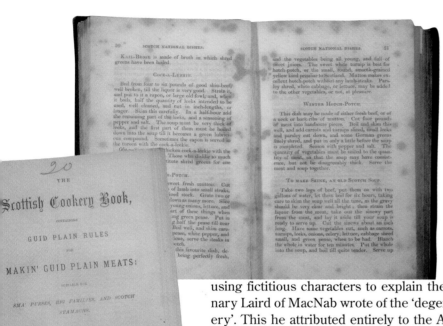

Andrew Stewart, The Scottish Cookery Book *(Edinburgh and Glasgow, 1878).*
Andrew Stewart's cookery books were unashamedly compiled to 'safeguard Scottish culinary traditions from further assault', with the blame being laid firmly at the door of the English. *National Library of Scotland.*

ANDREW STEWART, A JOURNALIST BASED in Dundee, felt particularly strongly about what he perceived to be the dilution of his national cuisine. His *Scottish Cookery Book*, published in 1878, was unashamedly compiled to 'safeguard Scottish culinary traditions from further assault'.[1] In its subtitle, the book claimed to be intended for 'Sma' Purses, Big Families, and Scotch Stamachs'. Stewart wrote 'Warne and [Mrs] Beeton's penny cookery books have met with great success in England . . . but to the Scotch people they are practically useless'.

Following Meg Dods's technique of using fictitious characters to explain the purpose of his book, Stewart's imaginary Laird of MacNab wrote of the 'degeneracy of Scotch men and Scotch Cookery'. This he attributed entirely to the Act of Union of 1707. Of the English he wrote, 'the vera sight of a haggis is eneuch to turn their stamachs inside out; and as to hotch-potch, and crappit heids, the puir ignorant creatures'. He continues, 'and our Scotch fowk are takin' after them – deil burst them! The feck o' their dinners made up o' jellies, tarts, and sic-like trasherie'.

In his preface, Andrew Stewart put out a call for like-minded Scots to send him more peculiarly Scottish recipes. So great was the response that he was able to publish a second cookery book along the same lines as the first. *The Thrifty Housewife or Plain Fare for Plain Folk* appeared a few years later. Stewart was a journalist on *The People's Friend*, a broadsheet popular with the ever-increasing ranks of the middle classes, and it was at these same people that his cookery books were directed.

One writer who would have been an easy target for Andrew Stewart was Sarah Reddie. The English-born wife of Major-General George Burd Reddie, Sarah's family home was in Fife. In common with many another army wife, she accompanied her husband on his postings abroad, notably to India. The family was resident variously in Lahore, Calcutta, and in the Punjab between 1847 and 1862. This cosmopolitan background is reflected in her recipe book, which includes many dishes gleaned from friends and expatriate acquaintances in India. The first

[1] Andrew Stewart, *The Scottish Cookery Book, containing guid plain rules for makin' guid plain meats: suitable for sma' purses, big families, and Scotch stamachs* (Edinburgh and Glasgow, 1878).

date in Sarah Reddie's recipe book is 1847, but she continued to make new entries until the mid-1880s.[2]

There are recipes for 'German Bread Pudding', 'Irish Marmalade', numerous Indian curries and chutneys, and a 'Swedish Pie' of lean beef, onions, herbs, and seasonings. 'Tomatoes à la Italien', a recipe for fried tomatoes buttered and seasoned with pepper, came to Sarah's notice while in Lahore in 1854. Tomato recipes are liberally sprinkled throughout the notebook. In addition to the Italian tomatoes, there are two tomato sauce recipes (one called 'Love Apple Sauce'). One of the first British tomato recipes is Hannah Glasse's recipe 'To dress Haddocks the Spanish way'. Even in the mid-nineteenth century few Scottish recipe books mention tomatoes, and Sarah's interest in them suggests that they were still a novelty. It was not until the twentieth century that tomatoes gained widespread acceptance as a salad vegetable.

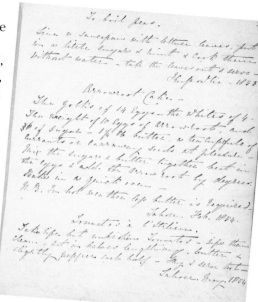

Salads, however, were becoming more widely accepted in Scotland. In 1826, Meg Dods had found them cool and refreshing: 'a harmless luxury when they agree with the stomach; and although they afford little nourishment of themselves they make a pleasant addition to other aliments, and to the dinner table'. Sarah Reddie's recipe for a chicken salad consists of chopped chicken, egg whites, onion and mayonnaise.

'Tomatoes à la Italien', from Sarah Reddie's recipe book, 1854.
Sarah Reddie accompanied her husband on many of his army postings abroad. Her recipe book reflects the cosmopolitan nature of their life and the influence of the British Empire.
National Library of Scotland, MS.5065, f.27.

CHICKEN SALAD

Mince up a cold roast fowl with the whites of two hard eggs and some onions finely minced, beat up the yolks with 3 teaspoonsful of mustard and some salt, then add 3 tablespoonsful of cream or salad oil 1 and 1/2 of vinegar a little essence of celery - mix all well up together and if salad is in season cut up some lettuce with it.

The influence of her English upbringing and of the British Empire is very much apparent in Sarah's notebook. 'Victoria Pudding', 'Victoria Blamonge' and 'Prince Albert's Pudding' are typical of many entries. Sarah's 'Victoria Pudding' recipe is for a pastry-based, layered dessert of jam and custard with a meringue topping. The source of the recipe was her friend, Captain Briggs.

VICTORIA PUDDING

Line a pie dish with puff paste, put a layer of preserve at the bottom, take 3ozs of loaf sugar pounded [ground], 3ozs of butter, 4 eggs taking out the whites - Mix all well together fill the dish & bake one hour then take the whites and beat them to a light froth put it on the top of the pudding a little before you send it to table - put it in the oven for 10 minutes to harden.

Cap. Briggs.

Sarah Reddie's cookery book includes many 'foreign' recipes which came to her notice because of the circles in which she moved. Such recipes were novelties, outside the normal run of her experience, and therefore of interest. However, from the sources she gives it is clear that many of her acquaintances in India

[2]National Library of Scotland, MS.5065.

Expressly Prepared for
Mrs Beeton's Book of Household Management

were Scots who were only too happy to exchange favourite recipes from home. So, there are recipes for Scottish dishes from minced collops to 'Oatmeal Cake', and from hashed mutton to 'Scotch Shortbread'.

A number of Sarah Reddie's recipes among those entered in the 1870s and 1880s are of particular interest for their layout. Listing the ingredients first and then stating the method, they have a familiar look today. At the time, this approach was novel. One of the first cookery writers to adopt this format was Isabella Beeton in *The Book of Household Management*, first published in 1861. Having considerable advantages for the busy cook as regards clarity, this layout was increasingly adopted thereafter.

One of Andrew Stewart's specific complaints was of the increasing number of desserts served in Scotland. He wrote, 'the very idea of a dessert would never have entered into the thoughts of a Scotch housewife fifty years ago'. He tempered his comments when he remarked that he did not consider desserts entirely harmful as they 'give a fulness and completeness to the dinner at very little expense'. Stewart also acknowledged the advantages of fruit puddings 'as a corrective in the way of a mild laxative'.

'Puddings', from Isabella Beeton, The Book of Household Management *(London, 1869).*
One of Andrew Stewart's specific complaints was of the increasing number of desserts served in Scotland.
National Library of Scotland.

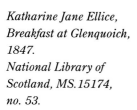

Katharine Jane Ellice, Breakfast at Glenquoich, 1847.
National Library of Scotland, MS.15174, no. 53.

101

From the 1870s, consumption of fresh fruit increased steadily throughout Britain.[3] Previously, the urban working class consumed very little fruit. This can be partly attributed to the continuing tradition that fruit was unhealthy and dangerous, especially for children. Even the wealthier classes considered it a rare and expensive luxury. This change in attitude was due to fundamental social, economic, and dietary changes.

While higher real incomes meant that fruit was more affordable for most people, the growth of larger urban centres created a ready market for such perishable foodstuffs. Improvements in transport provided the catalyst. In particular, the coming of the railways enabled producers to transport their goods at speed to the appropriate markets. In turn, production of fruit increased, although it must be said that this was so to a greater extent in England than in Scotland.

One of the criticisms levelled at Victorian cookery is of an excessive concern with the appearance of food at the expense of taste.[4] As in Victorian design in general, symmetry and form were all-important, and not the natural look of the foodstuffs. The result was a preoccupation with elaborate concoctions often achieved by the use of moulds.

Among the new desserts circulating mid-century were many based on chocolate. Drunk by wealthy Europeans since at least the 1660s, chocolate was consumed by the very wealthy in the form of chocolate almonds, chocolate puffs, or chocolate creams from about the same time.[5] The English cookery writer Hannah Glasse gave a recipe for chocolate creams in *The Art of Cookery* of 1747. However, it was not until the nineteenth century that chocolate was thought of as a food on any scale. It first appeared in the form of solid blocks in the 1860s. From this time on, the number of chocolate-based recipes attest to its popularity.

Sarah Reddie includes a recipe for a boiled chocolate pudding served with a vanilla sauce, given to her in 1860 by Captain Briggs, the source of so many of her recipes.

CHOCOLATE PUDDING

Boil a quart of milk, dissolve in it 1 oz of chocolate, sweeten with loaf sugar, add the yolks of 8 and the whites of 4 eggs well beaten. Strain and pour into a plain buttered mould steam it for 1/2 an hour: let it settle for 18 minutes and serve with the following sauce. Boil 1/2 a stick of vanilla in a pint of milk till it is reduced one 1/2. Strain, sweeten and thicken with arrowroot

Cap. Briggs 9/2/[18]60.

As the proportion of pudding and dessert recipes increased, conversely the number of preserving recipes declined. This is not to say that jam-making declined among the middle and upper classes in the nineteenth century. As is so often the case, manuscript recipe books reflect current trends in domestic cookery rather than actual dishes prepared. The rise in the proportion of dessert

[3] A. Torode, 'Trends in Fruit Consumption', in *Our Changing Fare*, ed. by T.C. Barker and others (London, 1966), pp. 115-34.

[4] Dena Attar, 'The Art of Dining in Middle-Class Victorian Britain', in *The Appetite and the Eye*, ed. by C. Anne Wilson (Edinburgh, 1991), pp. 123-40.

[5] Wilson, *Food and Drink in Britain*, pp. 364-6.

recipes reflects the increase in their importance and the appearance of new dishes. Although commercially produced bottled jams and preserves provided a cheap and ready store of such foodstuffs, only the poor purchased factory produced jam.

At the turn of the nineteenth century, the balance between recipes for preserves and desserts was redressed to some extent with the appearance of specialised cookery books.[5] Concentrating on the luxury preserves and delicacies made by the lady of the house rather than the everyday dishes produced by her servants, these works mirror, in many respects, the specialised recipe books of the seventeenth century, such as that from Dunrobin of 1683 and Lady Saltoun's notebook of 1688. These leisured ladies made preserves for their own amusement rather than out of necessity. Their products were delicacies which might be given to friends and good causes as luxury items.

Large-scale production of bottled sauces and preserves certainly contributed to the change in emphasis noticeable in many nineteenth-century recipe books. Another factor was the emergence of two new methods of preservation: canning and freezing. Pickling, salting, drying, and smoking had all been widely known for centuries and had dominated the national approach to food preservation, but the appearance of these two important new methods was to result in significant changes in the nation's eating habits.[6]

Metal cans were used for preserving food from at least 1814, when Sir William Parry took canned food with him on his Arctic expedition. In the process of canning, the half-cooked meat and liquid were placed in the vessel and the metal lid then soldered on. The can and its contents were sterilised by simmering in a salt solution. In Britain, canning was a commercial rather than a domestic operation. This was not necessarily the case elsewhere as some American cookery books give advice on home canning.

Canned food was not produced on a significant scale until the Crimean War. In 1861, Mrs Beeton wrote of large canning factories in Aberdeen and Leith. However, it was not until cans appeared on the shelves of high-street grocers towards the end of the nineteenth century that canned food became of real significance in the nation's diet.

The life-expectancy of a wide range of foodstuffs has been extended by chilling for centuries. James II had an ice-house or 'snow-pit' at Greenwich in 1662. Wealthy Scottish families had ice-houses on their estates from at least the eighteenth century. In these subterranean caverns, naturally produced ice was stored at below freezing temperatures and used domestically as a preservative. The fish-curing and shipping firm of John Richardson of Pitfour had experimented with exporting salmon packed in ice from the River Tay as early as the 1770s.[7] As a result of the potential losses should melting occur, this method carried a good deal of risk, and consequently ice was little used commercially in the eighteenth century.

[5] Lynette Hunter, 'Nineteenth and Twentieth Century Trends in Food Preservation: Frugality, Nutrition or Luxury', in *Waste Not, Want Not*, ed. by C. Anne Wilson (Edinburgh, 1991), pp. 134-58.

[6] H.G. Muller, 'Industrial Food Preservation in the Nineteenth and Twentieth Centuries', in *Waste Not, Want Not*, ed. by C. Anne Wilson (Edinburgh, 1991), pp. 104-33.

[7] National Library of Scotland, Richardson of Pitfour papers, MSS.20801-987.

The first scientific paper on refrigeration was produced in 1782 by William Cullen, then Professor of Medicine at Edinburgh University. The discovery in Siberia in 1799 of a frozen mammoth still in its original form and complete with grass in its stomach had caused much excitement: the potential of ice as the only preservative capable of maintaining foodstuffs virtually unchanged was realised.

From this time onwards progress was rapid. In 1807, advice on defrosting appeared in an English cookery book *A New System of Domestic Cookery*, written by E. Rundell. As published recipe books tend to reflect existing trends rather than establish new ones, freezing food is likely to have been common by then. In the 1830s, ice-cooled and refrigerated boxes became popular with the wealthy. The decrease in the number of salting recipes in cookery books of this time may be attributed to the increasing dissatisfaction with the nutritional value of salted meat and the growth in importance of freezing as a method of food preservation.

Precise 'Directions for Constructing an Ice house', including dimensions and a diagram, are given in the early nineteenth-century Kinfauns Castle Receipt Book.[8] An undated note in one of the Malcolm of Burnfoot recipe books states categorically that 'anybody that has a shady shrubbery can have an Ice-house without expense by heaping a large cone of well pounded ice or snow in the winter and causing it to be thatched with barley straw . . . In this way ice may be preserved for three years'.[9]

In 1877, the first practical mechanical refrigeration plants were in operation, fitted to ships carrying carcases of meat from America and Australia. Only a few years later, in 1881, New Zealand joined in the trade. From these small beginnings, the trade expanded rapidly over the next decade, flooding the country with cheap meat. The result was that meat, which had dominated the diet of the wealthy for centuries, was now within the reach of a greater proportion of society.

The nineteenth century was an era of considerable change in food habits, as in so many other aspects of British life and culture. Dining habits had been relatively static for centuries. The pattern seen at Saltoun in the 1720s and in Meg Dods's *The Cook and Housewife's Manual* of 1826 generally still held good. There, two similar courses both consisting of a large number of dishes were placed on the table and the diners either helped themselves or were assisted by servants.

This arrangement changed fundamentally in the second half of the nineteenth century. 'Dinner à la Russe', as described by Mrs Beeton in her *Book of Household Management*, was the new fashion. She wrote, 'in some houses the table is laid out with plate and glass, and ornamented with flowers, the dessert only being placed on the table, the dinner itself being placed on the sideboard, and handed round in succession, in courses of soup, fish, entrees, meat, game and sweets. This is not only elegant, but economical, as fewer dishes are required, the symmetry of the table being made up of the ornaments and dessert'.

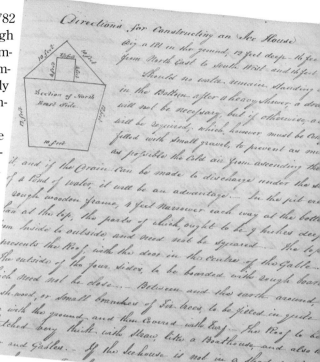

'Directions for Constructing an Ice house' from the Kinfauns Castle Receipt Book, early nineteenth century.

Ice-houses have been constructed on the estates of the wealthy since at least the eighteenth century. *National Library of Scotland, MS.24778, f.159.*

[8] National Library of Scotland, MS.24778.

[9] National Library of Scotland, Malcolm of Burnfoot papers, Acc.10708/1.

'Dinner Table with Floral Decorations. Arranged for 12 Persons', from Isabella Beeton The Book of Household Management *(London, 1888).*
In the second half of the nineteenth century, dining habits changed fundamentally. Dinner was now served 'à la Russe' with meals consisting of more courses and fewer dishes.
National Library of Scotland.

Meals now consisted of more courses and fewer dishes. Rather than the diners' plates being taken to the food on the table, the dishes were taken in turn from the sideboard and offered to the guests. The empty space on the table was filled with raised ornaments (sometimes candelabra), plants, or, as Mrs Beeton suggests, the dessert. Further ornamentation was supplied by the appearance of napkins folded into intricate shapes for special occasions. Decoration and appearance had become more important than the food served.[10]

The butler played a key role in the ceremonies which accompanied meals 'à la Russe'. As the servant in charge of the cutlery, he laid the table himself in a small household, while in a larger establishment this was done by the under-servants. The same applied to the silver and glass, and the table-cloth and napkins. The butler took full control of the meal as it unfolded, selecting and serving the wines, notifying the kitchen of its progress by ringing the dining-room bell, and placing and removing the dishes on the table as appropriate.

The privileged lifestyle of the wealthy Victorian household was in sharp contrast to the plight of the poor. As the century wore on, the quality of the diet of the Scottish working man, and particularly that of the urban poor, declined dramatically.[11] For centuries they had existed on nourishing broths, oatmeal, milk, and ale. In spite of the lack of meat this was a more than adequate diet. Contemporary surveys in Edinburgh, Glasgow, and Dundee reveal that these people now ate

[10] Attar, p. 134.

[11] R.H. Campbell, 'Diet in Scotland: An Example of Regional Variation', in *Our Changing Fare*, ed. by T.C. Barker (London, 1966), pp. 47-60.

largely bread, butter, and tea. Sugar had entered the diet of even the poorest agricultural workers. Their source of energy was the jam they spread on their bread. The hot part of a labourer's meal was supplied by mugs of hot tea, sweetened with yet more sugar.

The fears of Andrew Stewart, the author of *The Scottish Cookery Book* of 1878, that traditional Scottish cuisine would be swamped by that of a powerful neighbour is understandable. Surviving recipe books suggest that Scots were aware of the cuisine of other nations: they also point towards the emergence of a national British cuisine. However, manuscript recipe books tend to reflect what was new on the culinary scene as well as tried-and-tested recipes gleaned from friends and acquaintances. More representative of the national diet (at least of the affluent) are menus for actual meals.

The Edinburgh Skating Club claims to be the oldest skating club in Britain. It was clearly well established by the time its records begin in 1774. In the winter months, the Club held regular dinners, which became of great social importance in Club life. By the 1880s elaborately decorated, often humorous, menu cards were produced. As with so many such menus of the time, the fare is traditionally Scottish. That of 11 December 1885 lists oysters, cock-a-leekie soup, turbots and lemon sauce, haggis, sheep's head, plum pudding, and trifle.

The meals served to the dramatist James Bridie, while a medical student at Glasgow University between 1905 and 1910, are in sharp contrast.[12] Here, French influence is apparent with a 'Clear Julienne' soup, 'Mutton Cutlets à la Royale' and dessert of 'Trifle à la Chantilly'. Many of the dishes are more obviously English than Scottish. The quotations at the head of the menus are revealing: an extract from Robert Burns's 'Selkirk Grace' is followed by Shakespeare's 'Digestion wait on Appetite, and Health on both'.

English as well as Scottish writers denounced new methods of cookery, lamented the decline in standards, and complained of foreign influence. In the case of the English it was the French who were particularly derided, although American food habits were already creeping in. The nineteenth century was an era of change: always a difficult time. Whether some sectors of Scottish opinion liked it or not, Scottish society was increasingly cosmopolitan. Inevitably, Scots absorbed the cookery of the countries they worked in and visited. The evidence of cookery books, menu cards and accounts suggests that these imports co-existed alongside more traditional food habits.

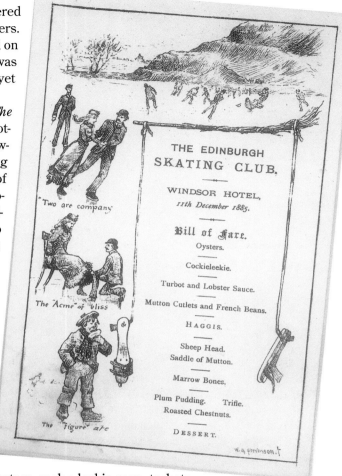

Menu card of the Edinburgh Skating Club, 1885.
In the 1880s, the Edinburgh Skating Club produced elaborately decorated, often humorous menu cards for its dinners. The fare served at the dinner on 11 December 1885 was typically Scottish. *National Library of Scotland, in MS.24641.*

---

[12] National Library of Scotland, James Bridie papers, TD.2229.

Menu cards collected by James Bridie, 1905-10. French influence is apparent in the menu cards for dinners served to the dramatist, James Bridie, while a medical student at Glasgow University. *National Library of Scotland, TD.2229/60. By permission of Professor Ronald Mavor.*

While new recipes were tried, tested and added to the repertoire, peculiarly Scottish dishes continued to be served into the twentieth century: Scottish cookery was strong enough to survive the onslaught. It was not totally swamped, rather it emerged enriched by the experience. After the melting-pot effect of the First World War, however, regional differences in diet were to become of lesser significance.

SELECTED FURTHER READING

Black, Maggie, and others, *A Taste of History: 10,000 Years of Food in Britain* (London, 1993)

Brown, P. Hume, *Scotland before 1700 from Contemporary Documents* (Edinburgh, 1893)

Colville, James, ed., *Ochtertyre House Book of Accomps, 1737-1739*, Scottish History Society, (Edinburgh, 1907)

Curle, Alexander O., 'The Kitchen and Buttery Accounts of the Earl of Angus's Household, in Glasgow and the Canongate . . . 1608', in *Proceedings of the Society of Antiquaries of Scotland*, 42 (1908)

Gibson A., and **Smout**, T. Christopher, 'Food and Hierarchy in Scotland', in *Perspectives in Scottish Social History*, ed. by Leah Leneman (Aberdeen, 1988)

Hope, Annette, *A Caledonian Feast* (Edinburgh, 1987)

Kay, Billy, and **Maclean**, Cailean, *Knee Deep in Claret: A Celebration of Wine and Scotland* (Edinburgh, 1983)

Leeming, Margaret, *A History of Food: From Manna to Microwave* (London, 1991)

MacLeod, Iseabail, ed., *Mrs McLintock's Receipts for Cookery and Pastry-Work* (Aberdeen, 1976)

McNeill, F. Marian, *The Scots Kitchen* (London and Glasgow, 1929)

Mintz, Sidney W., *Sweetness and Power: The Place of Sugar in Modern History* (London, 1986)

Moncrieff, Robert Scott, ed., *Lady Grisell Baillie's Household Book, 1692-1733*, Scottish History Society, Second Series 1 (Edinburgh, 1911)

Rance, Patrick, *The Great British Cheese Book* (London, 1982)

Reid, John, *The Scots Gard'ner*, ed. by Annette Hope (Edinburgh, 1988)

Whyte, H., ed., *Lady Castlehill's Receipt Book: A Selection of 18th Century Scottish Fare* (Glasgow, 1976)

Wilson, C. Anne, *Food and Drink in Britain from the Stone Age to Recent Times* (London, 1973)

Wilson, C. Anne, ed., *Banquetting Stuffe: The Fare and Social Background of the Tudor and Stuart Banquet*, Food and Society Series 1 (Edinburgh, 1991)

Wilson, C. Anne, ed., *The Appetite and the Eye: Visual Aspects of Food and its Presentation within their Historic Context*, Food and Society Series 2 (Edinburgh, 1991)

Wilson, C. Anne, ed., *Traditional Food East and West of the Pennines*, Food and Society Series 3 (Edinburgh, 1991)

Wilson, C. Anne, ed., *Waste Not Want Not: Food Preservation from Early Times to the Present Day*, Food and Society Series 4 (Edinburgh, 1991)

Wilson, C. Anne, ed., *Liquid Nourishment: Potable Foods and Stimulating Drinks*, Food and Society Series 5 (Edinburgh, 1993)

Wilson, C. Anne, ed., *Food for the Community: Special Diets for Special Groups*, Food and Society Series 6 (Edinburgh, 1993)

Wilson C. Anne, ed., *Traditional Country House Cooking* (London, 1993)

Yarwood, Doreen, *The British Kitchen: Housewifery since Roman Times* (London, 1981)

Index

Acton, Eliza, 88, 97

ale, 9, 13, 21, 97, 105

Alva House, 58, 61, 64, 68

Angus, William, 10th Earl of, 1-12, 13, 96
    household accounts, 1-13

Baillie, Lady Grisell, 38, 96

bakers, 4, 8-9, 35, 94

barley
    milling, 40

beer, 9, 21
    see also ale

Beeton, Isabella, 99, 101, 103, 104, 105

bills of fare, viii, 41, 87-88, 106

Boswell, James, 6

Bowland House,
    accounts, 92
    inventory, 85, 89-91

bread, 1, 4, 8, 9, 13, 68-69, 94

breakfast, 8, 24

Brereton, Sir William, 6

Bridie, James, 106-107

broth, 5, 6, 8, 11,22, 24, 25, 40, 47, 53, 62, 65, 76, 88, 105
    see also soup

Bruce, Katherine, Lady Saltoun, 31-32, 41
    recipe books, 31, 32-34, 35, 36-37, 103

Bruce, Robert, 15

Burnfoot, 71
    diary, 71, 80
    recipe books, 72-82

butchers, *see* fleshers

butler, 46, 90, 91

butter, 4, 23

Carberry Tower, 81

Carnegie, Margaret, 33, 35, 36, 38, 39, 40, 41

Castlehill, Lady, 19, 24, 51

Chamberlain, 20-21, 45

Chartres, Vidame de, 48

cheese, 4, 23-24, 28, 49, 97

cheesecakes, 65-66

china, 39, 90

chocolate, 102

chutney, 77, 78, 100

Cleland, Elizabeth, 57, 59, 62-69, 77, 79

coffee, 38, 97

cookery books *see* recipe books

cookery schools, 59

Coryat, Thomas, 15

crappit heids, 88, 99

Creech, William, 61, 67

currency, ix

curry, 77-79, 100

cutlery, 15-16, 46, 105

Dalrymple, George, 81-83

desserts, 28, 55, 75-76, 86, 87-88, 100, 101, 102-103

diet books, viii, 7-8, 23, 24, 25, 28, 43-45, 47-53, 55

dinner, 8, 24, 25, 41, 52, 86, 87-88, 104-105

Dods, Meg (pseud), 49, 77, 86, 87, 88, 94, 95, 97, 99, 100, 104

Douglas Castle, 4, 12

Douglas, Lady Grace, 73

Dudgeon, Mary
    account book, 60-69

Dumfries recipe book, 18, 19

Dundee, 99

Dunlop, 49

Dunrobin Castle, 15-29
    account books, 20-24, 25, 28
    Diet Book, 23, 24, 25, 28, 36-37, 52
    recipe book, 17-19, 20, 28, 103

Edinburgh,
    Argyle Square, 58
    Castle, 16
    cookery schools, 59
    George Square, 86
    St Colme Street, 89
    tradesmen, 4, 7, 61-69, 91-97

Edinburgh Skating Club, 106

Edzell, 17

eggs, 7, 8, 23, 51-52, 66

Elgin Pastry Book, 49, 54

Ellis, William, 5

Erskine, James, 58, 68

Erskine, Margaret, 57, 58, 61, 64, 69

Fettiplace, Lady Elinor, 27

fish, 2, 7-8, 22, 26, 36, 52, 63, 80, 93-94, 103

fishmongers, 61, 93, 94

fleshers, 61, 92, 93

Fletcher, Andrew, 32, 40

Fletcher, Henry, 40

food
    of the poor, vii, 4, 21, 47, 51, 53, 82-83, 97, 102, 103, 105-106
    of the wealthy, viii, 4-5, 11, 13, 21, 47, 51, 53, 82-83, 102, 103
    for visitors, 7, 10
    medieval, 4, 9, 15, 36, 46, 55, 65, 66

food merchants, 4, 37, 61-62, 63, 64, 91-97

food preservation *see* preservation of food

Forbes, Duncan, 74

Fowlis Easter, 44

French
    influence on Scots cookery, 26, 46, 93, 107

fricassees, 25, 41, 46, 49, 51, 64

Froissart, Jean, 9

fruit
    dried, 8, 55, 75-76
    fresh, 8, 16, 17, 55, 67-68, 94, 95, 102
    preserves, 17-20, 32, 33, 68, 74, 75
    recipes, 32-33, 74, 75, 76

fruiterers, 61, 94

Galashiels, 92

Galt, John, 74

game, 7, 10, 21, 25, 50, 52, 80

gardens, 16-17, 27-28
    see also kitchen gardens

Gerard, John, 27

Glasgow,
    household accounts, 1-13
    University, 8, 106

Glasse, Hannah, 60, 62, 77, 80, 100, 102

Gordon, Sir Robert, 16

Gray, Hector, 20-24

greengrocers, 94-95

grocers, 92, 94, 95, 96, 97

haggis, 26, 49, 88, 99

herbs, 8, 11, 14, 95

honey, 11, 24

household accounts, vii, viii, ix, 1, 2-13, 20-24, 25, 37-39, 43-45, 92-97

household inventories, 45-47, 85, 89-91

housekeeper, 46, 60, 91

house steward, 20-23, 45-46

Hudleston, Thomas, 82

ice-houses, 103, 104

inns, 12, 13

jellies, 33, 66-67

Johnson, Dr, 6, 21, 60

Johnston, Isobel *see* Dods, Meg

Johnston, Mrs, 46-47, 50, 51, 53, 59, 65

Keiller, James and Janet, 19

Kelso, 12

ketchup, 77, 79-80

kitchen equipment, 45, 90-91
  see also ovens

kitchen gardens, 16, 17, 37, 53, 55, 64

Kinfauns Receipt Book, 49, 104

Kitchiner. Dr, 76, 77, 88

Knockhill, 81

larders, 47

Lesley, Bishop of Ross, 2

Lindsay of Eaglescairnie, Mrs, 96

McLintock, Mrs, 32, 46-47, 59

McNeill, F. Marian, 26

Maitland, Sir Richard, 17

Malcolm, George of Burnfoot, 71-72
  family recipe books, 72-83

Malcolm, Stephana,
  diary, 71, 73, 80
  recipe books, 72, 74-81

marmalade, 18-20, 35, 75

Martin, Martin, 27, 48

Mary of Guise, 17, 26

Mary of Modena, 38

Mary, Queen of Scots, 18, 19, 24

meat, 4-5, 21-22, 25, 47-49, 62, 80, 92-93, 104
  preparation, 4-5, 25-26, 35-36, 47, 62, 93

preservation, 5, 6-7, 22, 48

Meikle, James, 40

menschotts, 1, 8, 13

menus, viii, 41, 87-88, 106
  see also bills of fare, dinner and supper

milk, 4, 7, 23, 95, 105

Milton, Lord, 39

Murray, Sir William, of Ochtertyre, 43-44

oats, 1, 8, 9, 13, 24, 68, 82, 101, 105

Ochtertyre,
  House Booke, 43-55
  inventory, 45-47

olive oil, 11

ovens, 8, 35, 45, 90, 91

Parry, Sir William, 103

pies, 34, 36, 50

Pinkie House, 17

pork
  prejudice against, 25, 33, 48
  sausages, 33-34

porridge, 24

potatoes, 27, 28, 53-54, 65, 81, 94

poultry, 7, 22, 34, 49-50, 62-63, 78-79

preservation of food, 5-7, 17, 18-20, 32, 33, 48, 51, 74, 80-81, 97, 102-104
  as an occupation for ladies, vii, 17, 68, 74, 81, 103
  see also fruit; salt; vinegar

Price, Rebecca, 19

puddings *see* desserts

ragouts, 25, 35, 46, 64, 94

Ramsay, Dean, 48

recipe books
  manuscript, vii, viii, 17-20, 24, 27, 31-37, 54, 60, 72-73, 74-81, 83, 99-101, 102, 106
  printed, vii, viii, 32, 46, 54, 59-60, 101, 104
  see also individual authors

Reddie, Sarah, 99-100, 101, 102

Reid, John, 27-28, 37, 53, 95

Richardson, John, of Pitfour, 103

rhubarb, 76-77

Robinson, Jean, 49, 54

Robinson, Thomas, 91

St Andrews University, 7

St Kilda, 48

salad, 53, 100

salt, 2, 5-6, 7, 22, 48

Saltoun Hall,
  accounts, 37-38
  barley mill, 40
  gardener's diary, 37
  menus, 41
  recipe books, 31-37
  rules for housekeeper, 60

sauces, 13, 20, 35, 51, 68, 77, 79, 80, 96, 97

Scott, Sir Walter, 59, 88

Seton, 14, 17

servants, vii, 20, 46, 60-61, 90, 91, 105
  food for, 28, 49, 51

shellfish, 36, 52, 63-64, 94

shortbread, 8, 96, 100

Smith, Eliza, 62

soup, 24, 62, 76, 77, 79, 81
  see also broth

spices, 11-12, 55, 78, 80

Stewart, Andrew, 99, 101, 106

Stewart, Margaret, 96

sugar, 11, 18, 66, 96, 97

supper, 8, 12, 24, 41, 52

Sutherland, John, 15th Earl of, 15, 23, 24, 28

Sutherland, Katherine, Countess of, 15

Tantallon Castle, 4, 10, 12

tea, 38-39, 41, 73-74, 95, 97, 106

tomatoes, 96-97, 100

Tweeddale, John, Earl of, 12

vegetables, 5, 8, 23, 25, 26, 27-28, 36-37, 53-54, 64-65, 80-81, 94-95

vinegar, 6-7, 48

vines, 16

Walker of Bowland,
  account books, 92-97
  inventory, 85, 89-91

Walker, Eliza, of Bowland, 85, 86, 89, 91

Walker, William, of Bowland, 86

weights and measures, ix

wine, 2, 9-10, 13, 21
  fruit, 74, 75

Yester, 12, 17